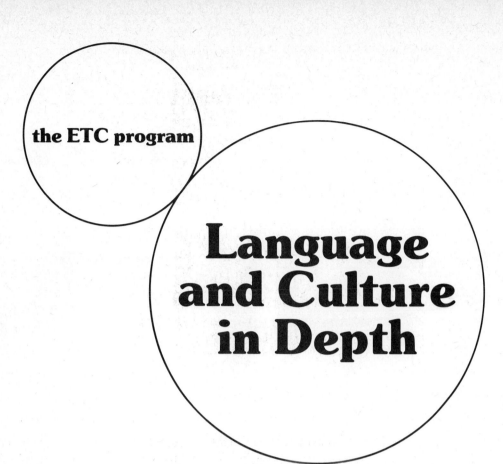

the ETC program

# Language and Culture in Depth

A Competency-Based Listening/Speaking Book

## Elaine Kirn
West Los Angeles College

RANDOM HOUSE  New York

First Edition

9  8  7  6  5  4  3  2  1

**Library of Congress Cataloging-in-Publication Data**

Kirn, Elaine.
    The *ETC* program. Language and culture in depth : a
competency-based listening/speaking book.

    Level 5.
    1. English language—Textbooks for foreign speakers.
2. Oral communication.    3. Listening.    I. Title.
PE1128.K4827    1989        428.3'4        88-29817
ISBN 0-394-35356-0 (Student Edition)
ISBN 0-394-35374-9 (Teacher's Edition)

Manufactured in the United States of America

*Series design and production: Etcetera Graphics*
                            *Canoga Park, California*

*Cover design: Juan Vargas, Vargas/Williams Design*

*Illustrations: Etcetera Graphics*

*Artist: Terry Wilson*

*Typesetting: Etcetera Graphics*

# Contents

**CHAPTER 8**    **Having Fun    85**

**Competencies:**  Expressing interests • Recognizing specialized vocabulary • Expressing, accepting, and turning down invitations • Understanding descriptions of sports events • Understanding and describing the rules of games

**CHAPTER 9**    **The Media    98**

**Competencies:**  Understanding and expressing opinions • Recognizing support for an opinion • Expressing opinions, agreeing, and disagreeing • Determining supporting reasons for an opinion • Summarizing the plot of a story • Debating issues

**CHAPTER 10**    **A Lifetime of Learning    109**

**Competencies:**  Recognizing the structure of a short speech • Giving a short speech • Recognizing ways to improve language skills • Understanding some views on language • Understanding rules of some common word games • Playing a question-and-answer game

# Preface

Language is me.
Language is you.
Language is people.
Language is what people do.
Language is loving and hurting.
Language is clothes, faces, gestures, responses.
Language is imagining, designing, creating, destroying.
Language is control and persuasion.
Language is communication.
Language is laughter.
Language is growth.
Language is me.
The limits of my language are the limits of my world.

And you can't package *that* up in a book, can you?

*—New Zealand Curriculum Development*

No, you can't package language in a book or even a whole program of books, but you have to start somewhere.

## About the *ETC* Program

*ETC* is a six-level ESL (English as a second language) program for adults who are learning English to improve their lives and work skills. The material of this level is divided into three books, carefully coordinated, chapter by chapter, in theme, competency goals, grammar, and vocabulary. For a visual representation of the scope and sequence of the program, see the back cover of any volume.

*ETC* has been designed for maximum efficiency and flexibility. To choose the materials most suitable for your particular teaching situation, decide on the appropriate level by assessing the ability and needs of the students you expect to be teaching. The competency descriptions included in each instructor's manual ("About This Level") will aid you in your assessment.

## About This Book

*ETC Language and Culture in Depth: A Competency-Based Listening/Speaking Book* offers two kinds of reading material: a personal story on the practical theme of the chapter and aural "realia"—simulated lectures or conversations from which students extract practical information.

Since high-intermediate students have the ability and the desire to express themselves on topics important to their lives, opportunity is provided for them not only to react to the stories and conversations they hear but to comment on the information and ideas in them and "tell their own stories." The pronunciation activities, while concentrating on features of speech, are geared toward the acquisition of notions and functions, such as asking questions to ensure comprehension, giving warnings, expressing opinions and preferences, agreeing and disagreeing, extending and reacting to invitations, asking and giving advice, and the like. There is also a large variety of conversation activities and games.

## Organization

Like most other books in the *ETC* program, this book consists of an introduction and ten chapters, each divided into four parts with specific purposes.

- *Part One: Learning to Listen* presents a personal narrative on the chapter theme, along with activities that develop students' ability to get the main ideas; pick out facts; recognize related concepts, relevant questions and answers, advice, reasons for a point of view; and other upper-level listening skills.

- *Part Two: Pronunciation Through Role-Play* begins with a conversation or strip story that illustrates upper-level pronunciation principles such as syllable and word stress, intonation, sound and word reductions, phrase reductions, sound linking, and sentence rhythm. Part Two progresses to pronunciation exercises and ends with role-play activities.

- *Part Three: Practical Listening* usually begins with everyday conversations or speeches on the chapter theme from which students are to make inferences. This part may end with "practical listening tasks" for students to react to by following specific instructions. There are also suggestions for "beyond the text" listening activities.

- *Part Four: Language Activities* offers a variety of conversation activities and games designed to practice vocabulary, notions and functions, and pronunciation principles of the previous three parts, while giving students the opportunity to express their ideas and enjoy themselves.

## Symbols

The following symbols appear throughout the text:

    activity on cassette tape

    **\*** a challenging beyond-the-text activity designed for more advanced students

# Available Ancillaries

A complete set of audio tapes accompanies this text. The instructor's manual for this text includes:

- a general introduction to the *ETC* program, this level, and this book

- general suggestions for teaching techniques to use in presenting the various kinds of activities

- an answer key for all text exercises with specific answers

- a tapescript for all material recorded on cassette

# Acknowledgments

To Etcetera, ETC, ETC, because we finally did it.

Appreciation beyond frustration goes to the many class testers and reviewers, reviewers, reviewers—whose opinions lie at the core of the *ETC* program. Thanks to the following reviewers, whose comments both favorable and critical, were of great value in the development of *ETC Language and Culture in Depth*:

Roberta Alexander, Saeed M. Ali, Carol Brots, Patricia Costello, Lorelei A. De Pauw, Marjorie S. Fuchs, Mary M. Hurst, Darcy Jack, C.A. Johnston, Gail Kellersberger, Dona Kelley, Renee Klosz, Kara Rosenberg, Saul Sanchez, Collins W. Selby, Cheryl L. Sexton, Jackie Stembridge, and Kent Sutherland.

The author wishes to thank the staff at Random House:
- Eirik Borve and Karen Judd—for keeping promises,
- Lesley Walsh—for being as efficient as ever,
- Marian Hartsough—for communicating where need be, and
- Cynthia Ward, Marianne Taflinger, and the sales staff—for what is yet to come.

Heartfelt thanks to the staff and supporters of Etcetera Graphics, Canoga Park, California:
- Joy Gilliam—for careful copyediting,
- Terry Wilson—for his inspired artwork and patience,
- Cindra Tardif—for expert typesetting, and
- Christopher Young—for alert and patient production,

and gratitude, appreciation, and love to
- Anthony Thorne-Booth—for his management, expertise, and hard work,
- Karol Roff—for helping, helping, helping,
- Sally Kostal—for jumping in to rescue us and to keep us calm,
- Chuck Alessio—for everything and more,

and to Andi Kirn—for putting up with it all.

E.K.

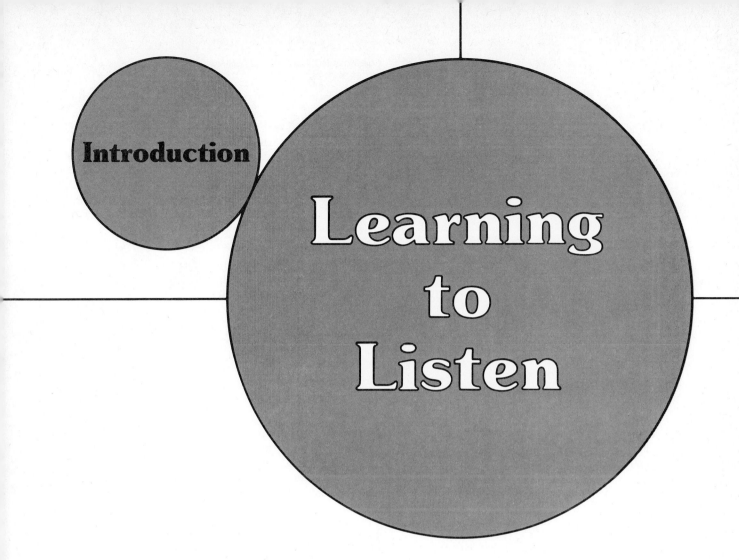

# Introduction

# Learning to Listen

**COMPETENCIES:** Understanding the characteristics of good listeners
Preparing to listen (discussing vocabulary and pictures)
Getting the main ideas
Making inferences
Understanding details
Telling your story

NOTE: Competencies listed above are reinforced in
all ten chapters.

### Preparing to Listen

If you prepare to listen to a story, you may be able to understand it better. Two ways to get ready to listen are to learn vocabulary and to discuss the pictures that illustrate a story before you hear it.

**A.** **Read the words and phrases. (You may want to pronounce them and discuss the meanings.)**

| **Nouns** | **Verbs** | **Expressions/Idioms** |
|---|---|---|
| boss | talk | changes the subject |
| expression | listen | paper clips |
| | interrupt | best friend |
| **Adjectives** | finish | pays close attention |
| impatient | explain | stay on the subject |
| | speak | |

**What do you think is happening in the pictures? To prepare to listen, make up a story about them with some of the above vocabulary.**

> ### Getting the Main Ideas
>
> The first time you listen to a story, you should listen for the main ideas—the most important thoughts. To get these main points, you don't need to understand every word or detail.

 **B.**  **Listen to the story. Then circle the letter of the one main idea.**

   **a.** The speaker is always changing the subject when her best friend needs to talk to her.
   **b.** The speaker's boss is a poor listener, but the speaker's best friend is a good listener.
   **c.** The speaker's boss never interrupts his workers when they ask questions or begin sentences.

> ### Making Inferences
>
> Instead of clearly stating the point (the essential meaning) of a story, a speaker may just indicate it indirectly. Then the listeners have to infer (figure out) the point for themselves.

**C.**  **To express the point of the story, write the missing words in this sentence:**

_____ listeners act differently than _____ listeners do.

**D.**  *Understanding Details*—In the story, the speaker describes the characteristics of poor and good listeners. Listen to the story again and write *a* or *b* on each line.

       **a** = characteristics of poor listeners
       **b** = characteristics of good listeners

1. _a_ They're often thinking about other things, not the conversation.

2. ____ They're impatient.

3. ____ They look at the speaker.

4. ____ They pay close attention.

5. ____ They show they're listening by the expression on their faces.

6. ____ They change the subject and don't answer questions.

7. ____ They play with something during the conversation.

8. ____ They help the other speaker stay on the subject.

**E.**  *Telling Your Story*—In small groups, discuss your answers to these questions. Then summarize your discussion for the class. (Tell what you talked about in a few sentences.)

1. In your opinion, do you listen well during a conversation? Why or why not?
2. How could you improve your listening skills?

**CHAPTER**

**1**

# Meeting People

| | |
|---|---|
| **COMPETENCIES:** | Introducing oneself and others |
| | Recognizing word groups |
| | Starting a conversation |
| | Making small talk |
| | Ending a conversation (leave-taking) |
| **PRONUNCIATION:** | Recognizing stressed syllables and words |
| **GRAMMAR FOCUS:** | Verb tenses (present and past—simple and continuous; future) |

# PART ONE / LEARNING TO LISTEN

● Introducing Oneself and Others   ● Recognizing Words Groups

## Vocabulary and Prelistening

**A.** **Read the words and phrases. (You may want to pronounce them and discuss the meanings.)**

| Nouns | Verbs | Adjectives/Adverbs | | Expressions/Idioms |
|-------|-------|------------|------------|--------------------|
| salesman | approach | complain | polite | native language |
| customer | pretend | shy | seriously | be married |
| speeches | smile | nervous | terrific | get up the nerve |
| note | prepare | attractive | perfect | take courage |
| envelope | practice | alone | coldly | get lost |
| accent | | blank | | have in common |
| | | charming | | |

**What do you think is happening in the pictures? To prepare to listen, make up a story about them with some of the above vocabulary.**

**B.**   *Getting the Main Ideas*—Listen to the story. Then circle the letter of the one correct ending for each sentence.

1. In his country, the speaker could easily ____.
   a. meet Americans and Canadians in hotels where he worked
   b. talk to anyone in his job and give speeches
   c. make small talk with women in laundromats

2. In this country, however, he feels nervous when he wants to ____.
   a. find out if he has something in common with a classmate
   b. write a long letter or make a telephone call
   c. approach Americans he doesn't know, especially women

3. The speaker's best friend met his future wife through ____.
   a. a personal introduction by a courageous friend
   b. a charming trick with a note in an envelope
   c. a telephone call to a number he found

4. Today the speaker finally got up the nerve to ____.
   a. greet a customer whose accent he couldn't understand
   b. approach a woman in a restaurant with a prepared speech
   c. invite an attractive model to have a cup of coffee with him

5. The woman, who was from the same country as the speaker, ____.
   a. told him to get lost
   b. smiled at him shyly and invited him to dinner
   c. made a good impression on him because she said nothing

6. Next time he wants to meet someone, the speaker will probably ____.
   a. prepare a long, polite letter first
   b. watch the person from across the room
   c. just introduce himself and start a conversation

---

### Recognizing Word Groups

Good listeners recognize meaning in phrases—word groups that express a thought. If you remember some important phrases, you may be able to retell a story even if you did not understand every word or detail.

---

 **C.**   Listen to the story again and retell it from this list of the important phrases.

not usually a shy person / job as a salesman
talk easily to customers / speeches in my native language
talk to American women / nervous about my English
don't know what to say

my best friend / approach an attractive woman in a hotel
clearly alone / wanting to talk to her for several days
wrote her a charming note / a blank envelope / walked over to her
careful, polite English / "I believe this letter...Your name..."
pretended that he was trying to read the name / "Kathy Johnson"
wrote her name on the envelope / handed her the letter
married six months later

got up the nerve / speak to a woman in a restaurant
prepared a terrific speech / practiced it in my mind
took courage / walked over / almost perfect English
my native language / accent from my part of the country
looked at me coldly / "Get lost."

the next time I want to meet someone
introduce myself / see what we have in common

**\*D.**   **In a few sentences, summarize the story in your own words. (Tell only the important ideas and events.) Try to explain the point. (Then you may want to read the note of explanation in the appendix.)**

**E.**   *Telling Your Story*—**In small groups, discuss your answers to these questions. Then summarize your discussion for the class.**

1. Is it easy for you to meet people? If so, where and how do you usually meet them?
2. Are you shy? If so, do you feel differently when you are speaking English than when you are using your native language? Can you approach men more easily than women, or vice versa? Why?
3. In your experience, what's the best way to meet people and make new friends?

# PART TWO / PRONUNCIATION THROUGH ROLE-PLAY

● Starting a Conversation  ● Recognizing Stressed Syllables and Words

 **A.** **Listen to this conversation. Then complete the items that follow.**

1. In your own words, summarize briefly what happened in the conversation.
   **Example:** Two men were talking at a party. The shy man wanted to meet a woman across the room.
2. Describe Frank's style of meeting women. How is it different from the other man's?
3. Try to explain the point of the story. (Then you may want to read the note of explanation in the appendix.)

---

### Syllable Stress

A syllable is a part of a word with one sound or group of sounds pronounced together (one "beat" of a word). Stressed syllables are pronounced more strongly (with more emphasis) than unstressed syllables. In some words, an unstressed syllable may seem to "disappear."

 **B.** **Listen to these words. An accent mark ( ´ ) indicates syllable stress.**

| one syllable | two syllables | three syllables | four syllables |
|---|---|---|---|
| job | coún try | eń vel ope | A mér i can |
| talk | lán guage | rés taur ant | sé ri ous ly |
| friend | po lite | at trác tive | in tro dúc tion |
| wrote | fi (nál) ly | pro dúc er | iń t(e)r est ing |

 **C.** **Listen to these words and write the number of syllables on the lines. Mark the vowel of each stressed syllable with an accent mark ( ´ ).**

1. _2_ pérson
2. ___ envelope
3. ___ careful
4. ___ front

5. ___ attractive
6. ___ honest
7. ___ introduction
8. ___ beautiful

9. ___ quiet
10. ___ flatter
11. ___ producer
12. ___ seriously

---

Not all words are stressed in phrases or sentences. Contractions with pronouns (*I'm, she'll, we'd, it's*, etc.) are usually unstressed, but contractions with *not* (*doesn't, didn't*, etc.) are usually stressed.

 **D.** **Listen to these examples of stressed words in phrases and sentences.**

my jób as a sálesman

lárge gróups of peóple

a blánk énvelope

her beáutiful eýes

I'm not úsually a shý pérson.

I couldn't tálk to ánybody.

I'd lóve to méet that mán over thére.

It's eásy to máke a goód impréssion.

**E.** As you listen to each phrase or sentence, write the number of syllables on the line and mark the stresed ones with an accent mark.

1. _7_ conversátions with wómen

2. _____ a charming note

3. _____ almost perfect English

4. _____ buy a cup of coffee

5. _____ Just flatter her.

6. _____ I can't give speeches.

7. _____ I'd like to talk.

8. _____ Ask if she's a model.

9. _____ I'll try it my way.

10. _____ What a nice introduction.

**F.** Listen again to the conversation at the beginning of this section (page 8). You may want to mark the stressed syllables with an accent mark ( ´ ). Then, in groups of three, read the conversation aloud.

**G.** *Playing Roles*—Pay special attention to syllable and word stress as you complete these activities.

1. Tell some phrases you could use to approach a classmate for the first time and start a conversation. Your instructor will list them on the chalkboard. **Examples:**

   Excuse me, could I please borrow a pen (a pencil, etc.)?
   Do you happen to have the time (change for a dollar, etc.)?
   Hello, my name is…(name). What's yours?
   What do you think of this weather (this activity, etc.)?
   That's a beautiful sweater (jacket, etc.).
   I've been wanting to talk to you for a long time. Can I buy you a cup of coffee?

2. For ten minutes, pretend there is a party in your classroom. Pick out four or more people you want to meet. Approach them with "an opening line" and try to make an agreement to talk later. (You might want to play the role of a shy person, an aggressive person, etc.)

   Have each person who agrees to meet you later sign his or her name here. On the second line, write the exact words of the "opening line" you used.

   NAME: _____
   " _____ "

   NAME: _____
   " _____ "

   NAME: _____
   " _____ "

   NAME: _____
   " _____ "

3. Tell your feelings about the introductions. Answer these questions:

   • Did you meet the four people you wanted to meet? Why or why not? Was it easy or difficult? Why?
   • Did you agree to talk later? Why or why not?
   • Which opening lines did you like best? Which would you use yourself? Why?

**\*H.**  Beyond the text: Approach three people you want to meet outside your class (Examples: at school, at work, in your neighborhood). Introduce yourself and begin a conversation.

Make notes on your experiences (the names of the people you met, the places you met them, and the exact opening lines you used, etc.). Then tell the class what you learned about meeting people.

# PART THREE / PRACTICAL LISTENING

● Making Small Talk

---

### Making Inferences

If you listen carefully to the speakers in a conversation, you may be able to make inferences about what they are saying. In other words, you might be able to make guesses or assumptions about the speakers' meanings or purposes.

---

 **A.** **Listen to Conversations 1–4. Match them with the pictures by writing the numbers 1–4 in the boxes. Tell the "clues" from which you inferred your answers.**

**EXAMPLE:** I know the woman and child had Conversation 1 because the boy called the woman "Mother."

**B.** **Read these sentences. Then listen to each conversation again and circle the letters of the two inferences you can make from it. (Don't circle the letters of the other statements, even if you think they are true.) Tell the reasons for your answers.**

EXAMPLE:    In Conversation 1, I guess the son has only one interest because everything he said was about money.

## Conversation 1

(a.) The son has only one interest, but the mother wants to have a social conversation about other subjects.
b. Andy wants to talk about movies, but his mother hasn't seen any lately.
c. It's winter, and the son doesn't like the cold weather.
(d.) It may not be easy for a mother and her teenage son to make small talk.

## Conversation 2

a. Two men who haven't seen each other for a while meet on the street.
b. They're both doing very well in business.
c. They don't know how to make small talk very well.
d. It's too bad they don't have more time for a conversation.

## Conversation 3

a. These students are new students.
b. One student wants to talk to the other while they are waiting in line.
c. She asks questions, and they begin an interesting conversation.
d. They may have interests in common, but they'll never know it.

## Conversation 4

a. The man may really need help with the washing machine, or he may just want to start a conversation with the woman.
b. She is afraid of him, so she gives him only short answers.
c. The man is married, so she doesn't want to get to know him better.
d. Some friendly small talk may become a conversation about more important things.

**\*C.** **Look at each picture on page 12 again and answer these questions:**

1. Who tried to begin the conversation? How did he or she begin (with a complaint, a question, a comment, etc.)?
2. Was he or she successful in making small talk? Why or why not?

# PART FOUR / LANGUAGE ACTIVITIES

● Using Expressions for Introductions, Greetings, Small Talk, and Leave-Taking

---

### Fixed Phrases

Most people use "fixed phrases" in introductions, greetings, small talk, and leave-taking (ending conversations). These expressions don't usually add new or important information, but they are polite, so they help people feel comfortable.

---

**A.** **Match these expressions with the situations in the four pictures by writing the letters *a–d* on the lines.**

**a.** an introduction    **b.** greetings    **c.** small talk    **d.** leave-taking

1. _a_ Silvia, I'd like you to meet a friend of mine, Jane Chu. Jane, this is Silvia, a classmate from school.

2. ____ Sasha sure gives great parties. Are you enjoying yourself?

3. ____ Well, tell me a little about yourself. What kind of work do you do?

4. ____ Sorry, but I have to run. Good-bye.

5. ____ Chuck! Long time, no see! How are you?

6. ____ I'd better get going. Nice talking to you.

7. ____ I'm fine. How about you? What's going on?

8. ____ Glad to meet you, Jane. I've heard a lot about you.

9. ____ Same here, Silvia. Nice to meet you, too.

10. ____ Nothing much. What's new with you?

11. ____ Have you seen any good movies lately?

12. ____ Well, so long. Let's get together some time.

**Now, in groups, cover the sentences and role-play conversations for the four situations in the pictures.**

**B.** The object of this game is to find out about the people at a "party" in your classroom, and the first player to complete the following list is the winner. To play the game, you will have to meet your classmates, make small talk, and end conversations. Find a different person for each item below and write his or her name on the line with a few notes.

EXAMPLE:  a: Nice weather we're having, right?
b: Oh, I don't know. I like the weather in my country better.
a: You do? Why?

Find one person who...

1. likes the weather in his or her country better than the weather here. (Why?) _____

    _____

2. wants to be a millionaire, a model, or a movie producer. (How will he or she do it?) _____

    _____

3. thinks women should take the first step in meeting men. (Why?) _____

    _____

4. has seen a good movie in English recently. (What was it?) _____

    _____

5. has a job similar to yours. (What is it?) _____

    _____

6. has interests in common with you. (What are they?) _____

    _____

7. likes American food. (What are his or her two favorite dishes?) _____

    _____

Summarize the most interesting of your "party" conversations for the class.

EXAMPLE:  Tova had a very interesting job in her country. She was an officer in the army.

**\*C.** Beyond the text: Meet two new people outside your class (Examples: at school, at work, in your neighborhood) or start a conversation with someone you already know. Find out what you have in common or learn something new about him or her. Then tell the class about the person.

# CHAPTER 2

# Getting an Education

| | |
|---|---|
| **COMPETENCIES:** | Making cultural comparisons about education |
| | Recognizing and answering "real" questions |
| | Asking questions and making requests in the classroom |
| | Understanding a class lecture (on the U.S. educational system) |
| | Recognizing chronological (time) order |
| | Matching details with main topics |
| | Understanding school customs and rules |
| **PRONUNCIATION:** | Recognizing sentence intonation |
| **GRAMMAR FOCUS:** | Question forms |

# PART ONE / LEARNING TO LISTEN

● Making Cultural Comparisons about Education    ● Recognizing and Answering "Real" Questions

## Vocabulary and Prelistening

**A.** Read the words and phrases. (You may want to pronounce them and discuss the meanings.)

| Nouns | | Verbs | Expressions/Idioms |
|---|---|---|---|
| system | assignments | address | make it on time |
| campus | quizzes | apologize | make up the work |
| instructor | finals | register | follow the instructions |
| culture | tuition fees | enroll | (not) feel like |
| lectures | process | drop | be used to |
| homework | | fail | midterm exams |

**What do you think is happening in the pictures? To prepare to listen, make up a story about them with some of the above vocabulary.**

**B.**   *Getting the Main Ideas*—Listen to the story, "Cultural Comparisons." Then circle the letter of the one correct phrase to complete each sentence.

1. The system of college education in the speaker's native country is _____ that in the United States.
   a. exactly the same as
   b. similar to
   c. quite different from

2. She thinks that she _____ her instructor in the wrong way.
   a. greeted and addressed
   b. answered questions from
   c. laughed at

3. Maybe she made another mistake when she _____.
   a. entered the classroom too early
   b. made up her work
   c. apologized to the teacher for arriving late

4. She feels _____ to ask questions about lecture points or instructions she doesn't understand.
   a. eager
   b. ready
   c. embarrassed

5. She's not used to _____.
   a. assignments and exams
   b. good grades
   c. textbooks and dictionaries

6. She already knows how to _____.
   a. explain the educational process in the United States
   b. register, enroll in classes, pay tuition fees, and drop courses
   c. find out what she needs to know

---

### Recognizing and Answering "Real" Questions

Speakers sometimes ask questions that they already know the answers to because they are looking for agreement.

**Examples:**

I made a mistake, didn't I?
Instructors know all the answers, don't they?

But usually a speaker really wants to know the answer to a question.

**Examples:**

How do students greet professors in your culture?
What should I do if I can't make it to class?

---

 **C.**  **Listen to the story again and pay special attention to the speaker's questions. Complete the following questions, which she really does want answers to.**

1. How do students usually *address their professors in this culture* ?
2. What do *they* do if _____?
3. If I don't go to class at all, how do I _____?
4. How can I follow _____?
5. Is it O.K. if I _____?
6. What am I going to do if _____?
7. Can I _____ ? How about _____?
8. How can I find out _____?

---

**\*D.**  **In small groups, try to agree on answers to the speaker's questions in Exercise C. Tell the class your answers.**

EXAMPLE:  How do students usually address their professors in this culture?

They use the professor's title and last name (**Example:** Ms. Nash). If a teacher establishes a less formal atmosphere, they might use his or her first name in or out of class.

---

**\*E.**  **In a few sentences, summarize the story in your own words. (You can look back at the pictures, if necessary.) Try to explain the point. (Then you may want to read the note of explanation in the appendix.)**

---

**F.**  *Telling Your Story*—**In small groups, follow these instructions. Then summarize your discussion for the class.**

1. Describe the educational system in your culture. Tell how it is similar to or different from that in the United States or Canada.
2. Ask your classmates questions about classroom customs and the educational process in this country. List questions to ask your instructor during the class discussion that will follow.

# PART TWO / PRONUNCIATION THROUGH ROLE-PLAY

● Asking Questions and Making Requests in the Classroom   ● Recognizing Sentence Intonation

 **A.**   **Listen to this conversation. Then complete the items that follow.**

1. In your own words, summarize briefly what happened in the conversation. **Example:** An instructor completed a lecture and then asked for questions.

2. Answer these questions: What does the instructor expect of his class? What are the students probably thinking or feeling?

3. Try to explain the point of the story. (Then you may want to read the note of explanation in the appendix.)

> Intonation is the rise or fall of the pitch of the voice in speech, most commonly beginning on the last stressed syllable of a sentence. It can be important to meaning. Rising intonation usually indicates that a speaker expects a *yes/no* answer (**Examples:** Yes, you can. No, I don't. Uh-huh.) or a short response to a request (**Examples:** All right. O.K. Sorry, but…). Falling intonation may mean that a speaker expects information, a comment, or no response at all.

 **B.** Listen to these examples. An arrow (  ) indicates rising or falling intonation.

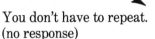

Are there any questions?
(No, there aren't.)

You don't have to repeat.
(no response)

Can you explain that again?
(Of course.)

Don't forget the homework.
(I won't.)

Did I speak slowly enough?
(Yes, you did.)

When's the next quiz?
(On Friday.)

You're late to class again?
(Uh-huh. Sorry.)

What does that word mean?
(It means…)

 **C.** Listen to these sentences. After you hear each one, circle the letter of one or two possible responses.

1. (a.) You can write a paper.
   b. Yes, you can.

2. (a.) What kind of assignment?
   (b.) All right.

3. a. When do we start?
   b. No, it isn't.

4. a. Yes, I do.
   b. O.K.

5. a. All right—for this quiz.
   b. Don't be silly.

6. a. You can use one.
   b. Yes, you do.

7. a. What did you mean by…?
   b. Yes, I have one.

8. a. At the age of four or five.
   b. Maybe.

9. a. Of course not.
   b. It's free.

10. a. Local government.
    b. They sure do.

> There are two kinds of tag questions (short questions added to statements). A speaker who really wants an answer uses rising intonation. A speaker who doesn't expect or want an answer uses falling intonation.

 **D.**   **Listen to these examples. An arrow ( ↗ ↘ ) indicates rising or falling intonation.**

You made a mistake, didn't you? (No, I didn't.)

I can take the exam tomorrow, can't I? (No, sorry, you can't.)

Some instructors lecture too much, don't they? (no response)

Today's homework assignment wasn't too long, was it? (no response)

 **E.**   **Listen to these tag questions and draw an arrow for the intonation of each.**

1. You understood the explanation, didn't you?

2. There isn't any homework for tomorrow, is there?

3. The writing assignment is due next week, isn't it?

4. We have to read twenty pages in the textbook, don't we?

5. There aren't any adult schools in your country, are there?

6. You don't understand everything the instructor says, do you?

7. You can tell us about registration and enrollment, can't you?

8. You're getting the point of all of these exercises, aren't you?

 **F.**  **Listen again to the conversation at the beginning of this section (page 20). You may want to mark the intonation of each sentence with a rising or falling arrow. Then, in groups, read the conversation aloud.**

**G.**  *Playing Roles*—**Pay special attention to your intonation as you complete these activities.**

1. Tell some phrases you could use to ask for information or to make a request. Your instructor will list them on the chalkboard. **Examples:**

   Can you tell us more about...?
   What should I do to + VERB...?
   Excuse me. Could you please speak a little more slowly (repeat the question, etc.)?

2. Several students prepare to play the role of "instructor" or "guest speaker" in the class by organizing short "lectures" on the educational systems in their countries or related topics. The other students will act as their "class." As the speakers give their talks in turn, they complete at least three of the following instructions.

   • Ask a student a question about his or her culture. (The question should be related to the topic of the talk.)
   • Ask if the class understands you or needs more explanation.
   • Ask a student his or her opinion.
   • Ask the class for comments, opinions, or questions.
   • Ask a student to answer another student's question.

3. If you are playing the role of student, complete at least three of the following instructions during or after the lectures. As you complete each one, check it.

   • Ask the speaker to talk more clearly or to repeat a point.
   • Ask the speaker for explanation of a point.
   • Ask the speaker what a word means.
   • Ask the speaker a question about his or her topic.
   • Ask the speaker about a homework assignment or exam.

**\*H.**  **Beyond the text: In your next "real" class, ask questions or make requests of your instructor and classmates. If you don't understand an answer, ask the speaker to repeat it or explain the point in another way.**

# PART THREE / PRACTICAL LISTENING

● Understanding a Class Lecture  ● Recognizing Chronological (Time) Order  ● Matching Details with Main Topics

---

> The formal description of a process usually follows chronological (time) order. The speaker makes clear which event or step comes first, which comes next, and so on.

 **A.** **Read these steps of the educational process in the United States. Then listen to the lecture, "Education in the United States," Parts 1 and 2, and number the steps in order. (Put 1 before the first situation, 2 before the second, and so on.)**

_____ senior high school        _____ an adult school, community college, or university

_____ nursery school        _1_ day care

_____ kindergarten        _____ elementary school

_____ junior high

---

> Many school lectures or other formal speeches follow planned outlines. If you listen carefully, you will be able to recognize the main topics and the details that explain each one. You can take notes on the organization of the talk.

 **B.** **Read the notes on the right. Then listen to Part 1 of the lecture again and match the notes with the appropriate topics on the left by writing the letters on the lines.**

1. day care             _c_

                           _d_

2. nursery school
   (preschools or playgroups)     _____

                           _____

3. kindergarten          _____

                           _____

4. elementary school    _____

                           _____

a. in many systems, seventh–ninth grades = junior high

b. private, community-sponsored, church-related

c. a few hours a day—parents work

d. baby-sitting arrangements—not formal schooling

e. offered free—schedules vary for budget reasons

f. readiness activities to prepare for elementary school

g. takes six to eight years to complete

h. first taste of sharing, following instructions

**C.**  Listen to Part 2 of the lecture again and complete these notes by adding additional important words.

1. Senior High School
   a. complete *twelfth grade* and graduate with *a diploma*
   b. may _____ after the age of ___ and start _____
   c. may take courses at _____ or _____

2. Community College
   a. _____ schools funded by _____
   b. low _____ for _____
   c. working adults can attend _____
   d. can transfer to _____

3. Adult School or Occupational Center
   a. _____ for an occupation
   b. can prepare for and take _____
   c. variety of courses: _____
   d. some charge _____, but others _____
   e. less expensive than _____

**\*D.**  Beyond the text: The next time you hear a class lecture or formal speech about a process, list the events or steps in order. If possible, list the main topics and the details that explain them in outline form. Then use your notes to review the lecture.

# PART FOUR / LANGUAGE ACTIVITIES

● Understanding School Customs and Rules

> Styles of teaching and learning may differ throughout the world and even in the various schools and classrooms of the United States and Canada.

**A.** How much do you know about school customs and rules at the various levels of U.S. or Canadian education? Answer each question with your opinion by writing a letter in the box: **Y** for *yes* and **N** for *no*. If you think the answer may vary in specific situations, write **M** for *maybe*.

| | elementary/ high school | adult school | college/ university |
|---|---|---|---|
| 1. Will a counselor help students to choose courses and decide on an educational plan? | ☐ | ☐ | ☐ |
| 2. Are there fees or tuition to pay? | ☐ | ☐ | ☐ |
| 3. Must students arrive in class on time and stay until the end of each class period? | ☐ | ☐ | ☐ |
| 4. Do students call instructors by their first names? | ☐ | ☐ | ☐ |
| 5. Do they stand up to answer or ask questions? | ☐ | ☐ | ☐ |
| 6. Do they have to attend every class unless they are sick or have an emergency? | ☐ | ☐ | ☐ |
| 7. If they miss class, should they bring a note with an excuse from a parent or doctor? | ☐ | ☐ | ☐ |
| 8. If they are absent, is it their responsibility to find out about and complete the homework? | ☐ | ☐ | ☐ |
| 9. Can students study or work on assignments with classmates? | ☐ | ☐ | ☐ |
| 10. Is it O.K. for parents or friends to complete their assignments for them? | ☐ | ☐ | ☐ |
| 11. Can they share their answers and opinions with classmates during a final exam? | ☐ | ☐ | ☐ |
| 12. Do they receive grades? | ☐ | ☐ | ☐ |

| | elementary/<br>high school | adult<br>school | college/<br>university |
|---|---|---|---|
| 13. Can they make individual appointments with their instructors to discuss their work? | ☐ | ☐ | ☐ |
| 14. If they're not doing well in a course, can they drop it? | ☐ | ☐ | ☐ |
| 15. Can a school director or instructor call their parents to discuss their grades and attitude? | ☐ | ☐ | ☐ |

**B.** In small groups, discuss your answers to the questions in Exercise A and your reasons for them. Tell the class which questions you disagreed on and why.

**\*C.** Circle the numbers of the questions in Exercise A that would have different answers in your culture. Tell a small group or the class which items you circled and why.

**\*D.** Beyond the text: Observe the customs and rules in your English class or another course. (The instructor may state some of them, but you will have to figure out others for yourself.) List them and discuss them in class.

**EXAMPLES:**    If students arrive to class late, they enter the room quietly and sit in the back.

The instructor calls on students to speak, but if no one else is talking, they don't have to raise their hands to ask a question or make a comment.

# 3

# Money, Money, Money

| | |
|---|---|
| **COMPETENCIES:** | Recognizing causes of financial problems |
| | Recognizing related ideas |
| | Understanding banking services and choices |
| | Discussing bank errors |
| | Requesting financial information |
| | Understanding financial advice |
| **PRONUNCIATION:** | Recognizing phrase intonation |
| **GRAMMAR FOCUS:** | Nouns and determiners |

# PART ONE / LEARNING TO LISTEN

● Recognizing Causes of Financial Problems   ● Recognizing Related Ideas

## Vocabulary and Prelistening

**A.** Read the words and phrases. (You may want to pronounce them and discuss the meanings.)

| Nouns | Verbs | Adjectives/Adverbs | |
|---|---|---|---|
| habits | gamble | unaware | accurately |
| balance | overspend | | |
| statement | record | **Expressions** | |
| income | charge | checking account | bank loan |
| purchases | repay | checkbook register | pay off |
| debts | manage | charge accounts | finance charges |
| possessions | borrow | credit cards | membership dues |
| interest | | | |
| fees | | | |

**What do you think is happening in the pictures? To prepare to listen, make up a story about them with some of the above vocabulary.**

**B.**    *Getting the Main Ideas*—Listen to the story, "Financial Problems." Then circle the letter of the one correct phrase to complete each sentence.

1. The speaker doesn't really have any bad habits except that he _____.
   a. overeats
   b. gambles
   c. overspends

2. One of his main problems is that he _____.
   a. doesn't balance his checkbook
   b. spends all of his income
   c. records check amounts in his register inaccurately

3. Last Christmas he _____ all of the gifts he bought for his friends.
   a. paid cash for
   b. charged
   c. didn't use a credit card for

4. He's going to have to get another job or sell his possessions to _____.
   a. repay a bank loan and interest
   b. open a new bank account
   c. be able to buy gifts for himself

5. But he's not worried because _____.
   a. he's managing his finances well
   b. he's from a rich family that will give him money
   c. he's joined an organization that teaches financial management

---

### Recognizing Related Ideas

Phrases that express equal, related ideas may be joined by connecting words such as *and, or,* or *plus.* To understand additional information, listen for the important details after these words.

---

**C.**    Listen to the story again and pay special attention to related ideas. Write the important words from the missing phrases on the lines.

1. I don't drink alcohol at all and *I seldom smoke* _____.

2. I never overeat, I don't gamble, and _____.

3. I accurately record the amount of every check I write and _____

   _____ by comparing it to the statement that the bank sends each month.

4. Last Christmas I either charged my purchases on my store charge accounts or _____

   _____.

5. Then I had to get a bank loan to pay off some of those debts plus _____

   _____.

6. I'm going to need another job, or _____ to repay that

   loan and the interest.

7. The membership dues (to the organization I joined) are high, but I can write a check or

   _____.

_____ **\*D.** In a few sentences, summarize the story in your own words. (You can look back at the pictures, if necessary.) Try to explain the point. (Then you may want to read the note of explanation in the appendix.)

_____ **E.** *Telling Your Story*—In small groups, discuss your answers to these questions. Then summarize your discussion for the class.

1. When or how can spending money become a bad habit?
2. Do you have a checking account? Store charge accounts? Credit cards? If so, when or how do you use these items?
3. Do you know people who overspend? If so, in what ways? How do they pay their debts or solve their financial problems?

# PART TWO / PRONUNCIATION THROUGH ROLE-PLAY

● Understanding Banking Services and Choices   ● Recognizing Phrase Intonation

 **A.**   Listen to this conversation. Then complete the items that follow.

**Customer:** I'm new in the city, and I need a bank account.

**Manager:** Certainly. What kind of account?

**Customer:** Excuse me?

**Manager:** Well, we have checking and savings accounts. There are passbook term accounts, time deposit accounts, individual retirement accounts,...

**Customer:** Oh, I'd prefer to start with just a checking account.

**Manager:** Fine. We offer regular and special checking.

**Customer:** What's the difference?

**Manager:** On a regular account, if you maintain a minimum balance of $300, there's no monthly service charge. On our special accounts we require no minimum, but you pay a fee for each check.

**Customer:** I'd rather have a regular account.

**Manager:** Will this be individual or joint?

**Customer:** Oh, it's just for me—an individual account.

**Manager:** How many checks?

**Customer:** What do you mean?

**Manager:** Would you prefer to order 250, 500, or 1000 personalized checks at one time?

**Customer:** I'd like 250.

**Manager:** Let's see now...our check holders come in three colors. Would you prefer black, yellow, or red?

**Customer:** I'll take red.

**Manager:** Okay. Now if you'll just wait a few minutes, I'll get you a book of fifty check designs to choose from. Then I'll need to ask you a few questions.

1. In your own words, summarize briefly what happened in the conversation.

2. Tell the choices that the bank offers (**Example:** a checking or a savings account).

3. Try to explain the point of the "story." (Then you may want to read the note of explanation in the appendix.)

> To indicate that certain words belong together, English speakers may use a slight rising or falling intonation and may pause briefly at the end of each group of words that expresses a thought. This intonation pattern helps relate the separate thought groups within a sentence.

 **B.** **Listen to these examples of phrase intonation. A horizontal line ( ‾_⌐_ _⌐ ⅃ ) indicates intonation and a vertical one ( │ ) indicates a pause.**

I don't gamble│and I rarely stay out late.

I don't drink│or smoke│and I eat and sleep well.

It's not that I'm unaware│of the balance│in my checkbook.

I accurately│record the amount│of every check I write.

**C.** **As you listen to these sentences, draw a vertical line for the pauses. (You may want to draw a line for the intonation pattern as well.)**

1. It's just│that│I always│spend│all of my income.

2. In other words, I can balance my checkbook, but is that what counts?

3. I'm going to need another job, or I'll have to sell off a number of my possessions to repay

   that loan and the interest.

4. Of course, I can write a check or charge the fees for membership dues on my credit card.

---

> In a question about two choices, the voice goes up (as in a *yes/no* question) at
> the end of the first choice and down (as in a statement or *wh*-question) at the
> end of the sentence. In a series (a list of items), there is a slight rising
> intonation on all but the last item.

---

 **D.** **Listen to these examples.**

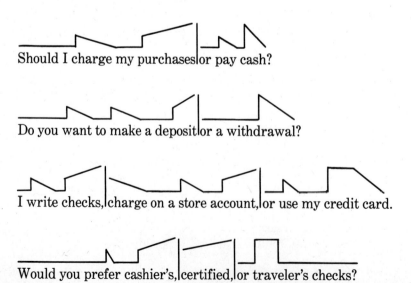

Should I charge my purchases│or pay cash?

Do you want to make a deposit│or a withdrawal?

I write checks,│charge on a store account,│or use my credit card.

Would you prefer cashier's,│certified,│or traveler's checks?

**E.** As you listen to these sentences, draw a vertical line for the pauses between thought groups. (You may want to draw a line for the intonation pattern as well.)

1. Do you want cash back in large bills|or small ones?

2. I'd prefer $50s, $20s, and $10s.

3. Are you applying for a personal or a real estate loan?

4. I'm not sure if I want a 12-month, a 24-month, or a 36-month car loan.

5. Will this be a regular or a special checking account?

6. I'd like a brown, a blue, or a red cover on my checkbook, but I'm not sure which.

7. Would you prefer to order 250, 500, or 1000 personalized checks at one time?

8. Are you opening a passbook, time deposit, or individual retirement account?

 **F.** Listen again to the conversation at the beginning of this section (page 32). You may want to mark the pauses or intonation of each sentence with lines. Then, in pairs, read the conversation aloud.

_____ **G.**   *Playing Roles*—Pay special attention to your intonation as you complete these activities.

1. Tell some phrases you could use to offer and make choices. Your instructor will list them on the board. **Examples:**

   Do you prefer (to + VERB)...?          Would you like (to + VERB)...?
   We offer both...and....                I'd rather + VERB...than + VERB....
   We'd prefer + NOUN to + NOUN.          I think I'll + VERB....

2. Six or more students take the roles of bank employees and choose one of the following kinds of information to give to "customers" (the other students). Each "employee" sits at a desk or table in a different part of the room. As the "customers" move from place to place, the "employees" explain services and ask them for their decisions. The customers answer and then circle the choices they make. **Examples:**

   **Employee:**  Would you like to make a deposit or a withdrawal?

   **Customer:**  I want to deposit some checks and withdraw some cash.

   **Employee:**  Would you rather have large bills or small ones?

---

**Everyday Transactions**

make a   { deposit
         { withdrawal

deposit  { checks
         { cash

receive cash back

$50s        $10s
$20s        $ 5s

---

2 | **Opening a Checking Account**

regular        minimum balance
special        fee per check

250 }                   brown }
500 }   checks          blue  }   cover
1000 }                  red   }

overdraft protection
(automatic line of credit)

---

3 | **Subsitutes for Cash**

cashier's  }
certified  }   checks
traveler's }

bank drafts (wiring money)

---

4 | **Opening a Savings Account**

passbook term account
(minimum interest)

time deposits  { 6-month
               { 12-month

individual retirement account

---

5 | **Bank Loans and Credit**

12-month    }
24-month    }   car loan
36-month or more )

personal    )
real estate }   loan
business    )

credit cards

---

6 | **Other Services**

safety deposit box
24-hour automatic teller machine

automatic bill-paying  { rent
                       { car loan
                       ( home loan

bookkeeping services

---

_____ **\*H.**   **Beyond the text:** At a local bank, get brochures and ask questions about the services listed in Exercise G. Make notes on the information. Then tell the class what you found out.

# PART THREE / PRACTICAL LISTENING

● Discussing Bank Errors ● Requesting Financial Information

> If you listen carefully to the words, stresses, and intonation in a conversation, you might be able to make guesses or assumptions about the situation.

 **A.**   **Read these phrases and sentences. Then listen to Conversations 1 and 2 twice. The first time, circle the letters of the place and the speakers. The second time, circle the letters of all the inferences that you can make from the conversation. (Don't circle the letters of the other statements, even if you think they are true.) Tell the reasons for your answers.**

## Conversation 1

*Place*
(a.) a bank
b. a business
c. a credit bureau

*Speakers*
a. a manager and an employee
(b.) a customer and a teller
c. a cashier and a financial counselor

*Possible Inferences*
a. The man tries to be accurate in financial matters.
b. The woman doesn't know how to add or subtract.
c. They agree on the figures of the bank balance.
d. He is upset, but she has a sense of humor.
e. It's not clear who made a mistake, but the teller will try to take care of it.

## Conversation 2

*Place*
a. a bank
b. a department store
c. a gift shop

*Speakers*
a. an employee and a customer
b. a manager and a salesclerk
c. a teller and a secretary

*Possible Inferences*
a. The store wants customers to open charge accounts so that they'll make more purchases there.
b. She wants to give a calculator to someone as a gift.
c. She isn't going to buy much with her new charge card.
d. She's happy with the situation, but he wasn't successful in his purpose.
e. A transistor radio with earphones is worth more than a calculator.

**B.** Look at the coupon to use for requesting financial information. Then listen to Conversation 3 and check the services you might want more information about. Listen again and then explain your choices.

### PLEASE SEND ME MORE INFORMATION ON THE FOLLOWING:

☐ Senior Class (for retired members)
☐ The Unchecking Account
☐ Automated Teller Machines
☐ Telephone Teller
☐ Real Estate Loans
☐ Equity Checking Loan
☐ Santa Saver Club Account
☐ Quick Draw Account (Line of Credit)
☐ Visa
☐ Automobile Mechanical Breakdown Insurance
  (Available through Golden 1 Insurance Services)
☐ Credit Life/Credit Disability Insurance
☐ Group Legal Service
☐ IRA Accounts
☐ CU Auto Club
☐ Other _____

_____
NAME

_____
ADDRESS

_____
CITY / STATE / ZIP

**\*C.** Beyond the text: Call a financial institution other than a bank, such as such as a savings and loan association or a credit union. Ask questions about its special services. Take notes on the information. Then tell the class what you found out.

# PART ONE / LEARNING TO LISTEN

● Recognizing Health and Safety Hazards ● Getting Factual Information

## Vocabulary and Prelistening

**A.**    **Read the words and phrases. (You may want to pronounce them and discuss the meanings.)**

| Nouns | Verbs | Adjectives | Expressions/Idioms |
|---|---|---|---|
| protection | inform | outdated | union representative |
| conditions | complain | pregnant | safety hazards |
| vision | claim | hazardous | video display terminal |
| supervisor | stare | malfunctioning | dizzy spells |
| equipment | refuse | embarrassed | chemical fumes |
| transfer | replace | | x-ray technician |
| personnel | insist | | doses of radiation |
| protest | expose | | government agency |
| permission | contact | | paint solvents |
| management | inspect | | assembly line |
| fiberglass | prevent | | first aid |
| | | | rashes and itching |

**What do you think is happening in the pictures? To prepare to listen, make up a story about them with some of the above vocabulary.**

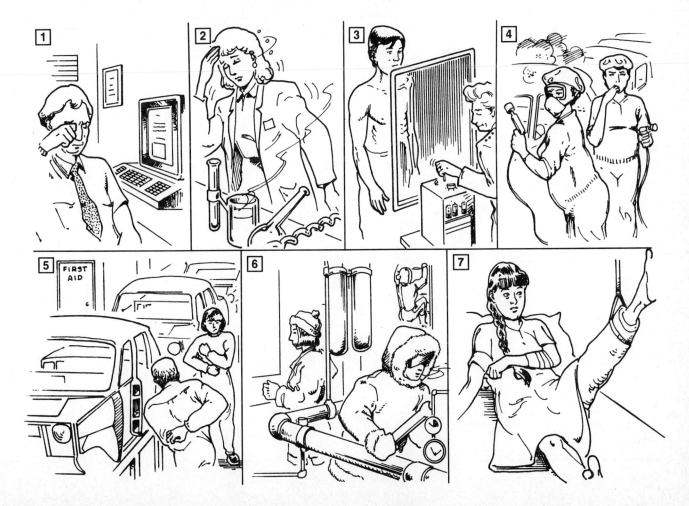

**B.**    *Getting the Main Ideas*—**Listen to the story "Health and Safety Conditions on the Job." Then circle the letter of the one correct ending for each sentence.**

1. Workers have a right to complain and try to get something done about _____.
   a. the use of computers by management
   b. health and safety hazards in the work place
   c. union representatives and inspectors from OSHA

2. If the management refuses to take care of a health or safety problem, it might be necessary to _____.
   a. contact the Occupational Safety and Health Administration
   b. organize a protest of some kind
   c. both of the above

3. The speaker doesn't have to worry about working conditions for a while because _____.
   a. the heating system is no longer malfunctioning
   b. she was fired from her job for complaining
   c. she had an accident at home that keeps her from working

---

### Recognizing Factual Information

The purpose of some stories is to inform listeners of facts. The information these facts provide is the important part of the story.

---

 **C.**    **Read these sentence beginnings. Then listen to the story again and pay special attention to the factual information. Write the important words on the lines to complete these informative statements.**

1. A union representative may visit a company to _____
   _____.

2. Workers who stare at a video display terminal for many hours might claim to _____
   _____.

3. Laboratory workers might get headaches or dizzy spells because it can be dangerous to
   _____

4. It's important to replace outdated x-ray equipment because it may be _____
   _____.

5. Pregnant workers must be careful to do everything possible to _____
   _____.

6. It's not uncommon for fiberglass to cause _____.

_____ **\*D.** In one sentence each, summarize each of the six examples of work-related health or safety problems from the story. (You can look back at the first six pictures, if necessary.)

_____ **E.** *Telling Your Story*—In small groups, discuss your answers to these questions. If possible, give specific examples from your personal experience or that of people you know. Then summarize your discussion for the class.

1. What are some possibly dangerous work conditions or safety hazards? How could they be damaging?
2. If you are worried about a particular situation, what can you do about it?
3. Why might some workers be afraid or unwilling to protest unsafe working conditions?

# PART TWO / PRONUNCIATION THROUGH ROLE-PLAY

● Understanding Safety Measures ● Recognizing Sound and Word Reductions

 **A.**   **Listen to these conversations. Then complete the items that follow.**

## Conversation 1

**Supervisor:** I hate to tell you this, but you're not supposed to wear any rings, bracelets, necklaces, or earrings to work. They could get caught in the machinery.

**Employee:** We can't wear any jewelry? Okay.

## Conversation 2

**Worker:** On this job, we've got to wear gloves and a mask.

**Coworker:** I know we have to use gloves to avoid touching the chemicals. But why is it necessary to wear a mask?

**Worker:** To protect our lungs from the fumes.

## Conversation 3

**Manager:** To prevent accidents, it's important to stack boxes straight—one on top of the other. And I want you to keep drawers closed, too.

**Employee:** Right. It was careless of me not to close them.

**Manager:** And it's essential not to block the fire exit.

**Employee:** Sorry. I'm going to move the boxes now.

## Conversation 4

**Worker:** What happened to cause the fire?

**Coworker:** I wasn't paying attention to what I was doing, and I guess I left the gasoline can next to the heater.

**Worker:** I'm glad to hear no one was hurt, but the boss told you not to store flammable supplies near the heat. You've got to be more careful.

   1. In your own words, summarize briefly the safety problems in the four pictures.

   2. All of the "stories" make the same point. Try to explain what that point is. (Then you may want to read the note of explanation in the appendix.)

> In a word of more than one syllable, the vowel sound in the syllable with the primary (strongest) stress is pronounced more clearly, longer, and with a higher pitch than the others. If there are any syllables with secondary stress, those vowel sounds are pronounced clearly but more quickly and with a lower pitch. All other syllables contain unclear, "reduced" vowel sounds, pronounced as neutral sounds in the middle of the mouth.

 **B.** Listen to these examples of stressed syllables and reductions. An accent mark ( ´ ) indicates primary stress. A line ( ╱ ) through a vowel or vowels indicates an unclear, reduced vowel sound.

| two syllables | three syllables | four or more syllables |
|---|---|---|
| ún ion | pro téc tions | sú per vi sor |
| vi´ sion | com pláin ing | de vél op ing |
| díz zy | em ploy ées | láb (o) ra to ry |
| cón tact | tér mi nal | rep re sén ta tive |
| sup pliés | góv ern ment | un nec es sár i ly |

 **C.** As you listen to each word, mark the vowel of the syllable with primary stress with an accent mark. Cross out the reduced vowels of the unstressed syllables with a line.

1. sólvents
2. damage
3. agency
4. assembly
5. organize
6. administration
7. experiencing
8. hazardous

9. embarrassed
10. malfunctioning
11. personnel
12. department
13. radiation
14. unusual
15. machinery

> The vowel sound of many short, very common words (*a, an, the, and, in, or, for, you,* etc.) is reduced in phrases and sentences to an unclear, neutral sound. The word *to* may sound like "du," and some phrases with *to* sound like one word (**Examples:** have to = "hafta"; has to = "hasta"; got to = "gotta"; ought to = "otta"; going to = "gonna").

**D.** **Listen to these examples of reductions. A line (  ╱  ) through a vowel indicates an unclear, reduced vowel sound in a short word.**

have tø ("hafta") go tø work

has tø ("hasta") use equipment

work før ∕ technician ∕n ∕ lab

going tø ("gonna") get ∕ job

ought tø ("otta") be careful

experience rashes ør itching

I hate tø tell you this, but jewelry gets caught ∕n thø machine.

You're not supposed tø ("supozta") wear earrings ∕nd bracelets.

We've got tø ("gotta") wear gloves, rubber aprons, ∕nd goggles.

**E.** **Listen to each phrase or sentence. Cross out the reduced vowels of the short, unstressed words with a line.**

1. have tø get ∕n apron

2. at a factory in the area

3. protect the eyes from sparks

4. careful not to cause a fire

5. Why is it necessary to wear goggles and ear protectors?

6. To prevent fires, you're going to replace all the worn wires.

7. And I've got to be careful not to overload the circuits.

8. It was careless of me not to turn off the machine.

9. You ought to cover containers with oily rags in them.

10. I'm not supposed to touch electrical equipment with wet hands.

**F.** **Listen again to the conversations at the beginning of this section (page 44). You may want to mark the syllables with primary stress with an accent mark and cross out the reduced, unclear vowels with a line. Then, in pairs or groups, read the conversations aloud.**

**G.**    *Playing Roles*—Pay special attention to primary stress and reduced vowels as you complete these activities.

1. Tell some phrases you could use to express safety rules or warnings. Your instructor will list them on the board. **Examples:**

You've got to + VERB....         It's essential to + VERB....

Sorry to have to tell you this, but you're (not) supposed to + VERB....

2. In pairs, have a conversation for each of these situations. You can use the words under the pictures.

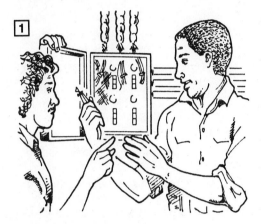

not supposed to overload the circuits
be careful to replace worn cords / cause
    electric shock or fire

wear a rubber apron and goggles
avoid unnecessary exposure to radiation
protect the eyes from flying objects

prevent accidents
turn off machines before cleaning them
not touch electrical equipment while
    standing in water

not smoke around flammable materials
cover the container with oily rags in it
be more careful

**\*H.**    Beyond the text: In pairs or groups, ask and answer these questions about health and safety conditions at your school or place of work.

1. What safety measures do students or workers take to prevent dangerous situations or accidents?
2. Have there been any accidents? If so, what caused them?

# PART THREE / PRACTICAL LISTENING

● Understanding Workers' Rights

 **A.** **Read these phrases and sentences. Then listen to Conversation 1 twice. The first time, circle the letters of the place and the speakers. The second time, circle the letters of all the inferences you can make from the conversation. (Don't circle the letters of the other statements, even if you think they are true.) Tell the reasons for your answers.**

*Place*

a. an x-ray laboratory
b. a first-aid room
c. the office of the hospital administration

*Speakers*

a. two computer technicians
b. a lab technician and a union rep
c. the head administrator of a hospital and a doctor

*Possible Inferences*

a. Old, outdated x-ray machines present a particularly dangerous health hazard to pregnant workers.
b. This hospital is going to buy new equipment because it puts the safety of its workers first.
c. If the woman makes an effort to complain about dangerous conditions or refuses to work, she could lose her job.
d. The union will force the hospital management to transfer the woman to an office job at higher pay right away.
e. Legally, employees have the right to refuse to work under unsafe conditions if the case meets the requirements of OSHA or NCRA.
f. Employees fired for certain reasons may be able to get their jobs back with back pay, but the fight could take a long time.

 **B.** **Read these sentences. Then listen to Conversation 2 and circle the number of the main idea (the most important information). Listen again to check your answers.**

1. Your employer will pay you if you have a work-related illness but not if you have an accident at work.
2. It's dangerous to lift a lot of boxes if the floor is wet.
3. If you are injured at work, you may get worker's compensation benefits from your employer's insurance company or a state agency.

 **\*C.** **Beyond the text: From the state employment office in your area or government agencies such as OSHA, get information about workers' rights. You might also get forms to fill out (Example: a claims form for unemployment insurance benefits). Have conversations with classmates about the available services. Then, in pairs, fill out the forms with information your partner gives you.**

# PART FOUR / LANGUAGE ACTIVITIES

● Getting along with Coworkers

> Many of the problems people have at work involve supervisors or other
> employees—in other words, getting along with other workers is very
> important to job satisfaction.

## A.

In small groups, read these paragraphs about typical work-related problems and tell
your personal opinions and advice. Try to agree on one solution for each problem. In
turn, the groups will summarize their solutions briefly for the class and the instructor
will summarize the solutions on the chalkboard. When all the groups have spoken, the
class will vote on the best solution for each problem.

1. In the firm where I work, I am one of the few women in charge of a department. My
   problem is supervising the employees. A few of the younger ones seem reluctant or
   unwilling to follow my orders, so I'm trying to state my instructions politely as requests,
   such as "Would you please do this?," or as offers to share the work, such as "I'll take care
   of this if you'll do that." Unfortunately, this solution doesn't seem to work, and I don't
   know how to handle the situation because I don't have the power to hire or fire workers.
   I'm afraid I'll lose my job if I can't get these employees to do the necessary work.

2. Most of the employees in my office seem to be working very hard, but one of the women
   is either slow and inefficient or simply lazy. While all of the others are doing what
   they're supposed to, I've seen her making phone calls to friends and relatives, writing
   letters, and taking care of personal business during working hours. The boss doesn't
   seem to notice, but it's difficult for the rest of us to complete assignments on time when
   she isn't doing her share. I don't like to cause trouble, but it isn't fair for her to be getting
   the same pay as we are when she's not doing the same work.

3. I don't have many interests in common with my coworkers, so I haven't really made
   friends with any of them. I don't want to pretend to be someone I'm not, but I don't like
   being left out of socializing in the work place, either. How can I find a way to fit in
   without appearing "phony"?

   **(When the exercise has been completed, you may want to read the suggested
   solutions to the above problems in the appendix.)**

## *B.

Beyond the text: In writing, describe a problem that you or someone you know has
had or is having at work. Your instructor will collect the papers, mix them up, and pass
them out to other students. In small groups, read and discuss the letters students in
your group receive and decide on the best solution for each problem. Write a
summary of the solution at the bottom of the letter you received. Your instructor will
then return the letters, along with the answers, to the original writers. Finally, students
in turn will then summarize their problems, the suggested solutions, and their
opinions of the advice for the class.

CHAPTER

# 5

# Getting Help

**COMPETENCIES:** Recognizing appropriate situations for legal self-help
Taking appropriate steps after an accident
Recognizing answers to common questions
Determining whether or not you need a lawyer
Understanding how small claims courts function
Understanding legal thinking

**PRONUNCIATION:** Recognizing phrase reductions

**GRAMMAR FOCUS:** The perfect tenses (present and past, simple and continuous)

# PART ONE / LEARNING TO LISTEN

● Recognizing Appropriate Situations for Legal Self-Help ● Taking Appropriate Steps after an Accident ● Recognizing Answers to Common Questions

## Vocabulary and Prelistening

**A.** **Read the words and phrases. (You may want to pronounce them and discuss the meanings.)**

| Nouns | Verbs | Expressions/Idioms |
|---|---|---|
| lawyer | handle | personal injury |
| injuries | settle | settlement money |
| attorney | exchange | contingency basis |
| client | tow | scene of the accident |
| insurance | rear-end | emergency room |
| fault | diagnose | collision coverage |
| whiplash | reimburse | repair shop |
| estimates | charge | claims adjuster |
| reimbursement | contact | pain and suffering |
| wages | recover | medical treatment |

**What do you think is happening in the pictures? To prepare to listen, make up a story about them with some of the above vocabulary.**

**B.**    *Getting the Main Ideas*—Listen to the story, "Legal Self-Help." Then circle the letter of the one correct phrase to complete each sentence.

1. If attorneys handle cases on a contingency basis (getting money only if they win), they generally _____.
    a. lose the cases
    b. receive a large percentage of the settlement payment
    c. advise clients to take care of the matters themselves

2. If there is a lot of damage in an accident, the drivers should _____.
    a. disagree on whose fault it was
    b. get a police officer to file a report
    c. move their cars out of the way of traffic immediately

3. In most states, the insurance company of the driver who _____ generally pays most of the expenses and damages.
    a. has the largest car
    b. can least afford to pay
    c. was at fault in the accident

4. To get compensation for pain and suffering and lost wages, the victim of an accident should _____.
    a. be examined by doctors and get a full medical report
    b. receive the highest possible estimate on car repairs
    c. both of these

5. An accident victim, especially one who was not at fault, may get _____.
    a. reimbursement for medical costs and car repairs
    b. compensation for pain and suffering
    c. both of these

---

> ### Recognizing Answers to Common Questions
>
> The purpose of some stories is to answer common questions that listeners might be asking. These important details give practical information.

 **C.** **Read these questions. Then listen to the story again and pay special attention to the details from which you can infer the answers. Write the important words on the lines to completee the answers.**

1. What kind of attorney might take cases that involve traffic accidents?

   A _____ lawyer.

2. In what situation might you try to handle the matter of a car accident yourself?

   If _____.

3. When do most lawyers agree to take a case on a contigency basis?

   When the case is _____.

4. If they can, what should the drivers do immediately after an accident?

   They should _____.

5. Why does a police officer come out to the scene of an accident?

   To _____.

6. If a car is rear-ended, what injury is the driver likely to have?

   _____.

7. In what situation might a driver who was not at fault in an accident choose not to contact his or her own insurance company?

   If _____.

8. What should he or she send to the claims department of the other driver's insurance firm?

   Two _____.

9. What else can he or she charge the insurance company for?

   The cost of _____.

10. When should he or she contact the claims adjuster?

    When _____.

**\*D.** **In a few sentences, summarize the story in your own words. (You can look back at the pictures, if necessary.) Try to explain the point. (Then you may want to read the note of explanation in the appendix.)**

**F.** *Telling Your Story*—**In small groups, take turns describing an accident you have had or seen or make up an imaginary accident. Discuss whose fault each accident was and the steps the drivers should have followed. Then summarize your discussion for the class.**

# PART TWO / PRONUNCIATION THROUGH ROLE-PLAY

● Determining Whether or Not You Need a Lawyer  ● Recognizing Phrase Reductions

 **A.**   **Listen to Conversation 1.**

### Conversation 1

**Hong:** Why do you look so tired? You ought to get more sleep. What did you do last night?

**Ruggiero:** Uh…I spent it in jail.

**Rafael:** What did you say? What are you talking about?

**Ruggiero:** I don't want to talk about it.

**Giovanna:** What do you mean? We've got to know what happened. Couldn't you tell us?

**Ruggiero:** O.K. I'm going to tell you, but only so that you don't get into the same kind of trouble yourselves. On my way home last night I was driving about ten miles over the speed limit, and—wouldn't you know it?—a police officer stopped me.

**Rafael:** So? I have to admit I don't know all the laws, but I know they're not going to put you in jail just for a minor traffic violation.

**Ruggiero:** Would you wait a minute? Evidently, every officer has to check your record on the computer, and this guy found out I hadn't paid the fines on several parking tickets.

**Hong:** Do you mean to say that you can be arrested for not taking care of parking tickets?

**Rafael:** What are you going to do? Do you have to hire a lawyer?

**Ruggiero:** I don't know, but I sure want to find out. I'm going to call the legal aid society to get some information.

**Summarize what happened in your own words. Try to explain the point of the story. (Then you may want to read the note of explanation in the appendix.)**

> In rapid, informal speech, some common phrases may sound quite different from the same words pronounced slowly and clearly (**Examples:** want to = "wanna"; don't know = "dunno"; what do you/what are you = "waddaya"; what you = "wacha"). You may not want to use these reduced forms in your own speech and you should never write them, but you should be able to understand them.

**B.**   **Listen to Conversation 2. Write the full words for the reduced forms of phrases in the blanks.**

### Conversation 2

**Clerk:** Legal Aid.

**Ruggiero:** Hello. I was arrested last night and I _don't know_ what to do.
1.
I thought I _____ _____ call to get some information.
      2.

**Clerk:** Certainly. _____ _____ _____ _____ _____
      3.               4.
know?

**Ruggiero:** In what cases _____ _____ _____ _____ hire a
          5.              6.
lawyer?

**Clerk:** If you've been charged with a criminal offense, you're _____
                                                        7.
_____ need legal representation.

**Ruggiero:** Do you mean that an attorney _____ _____ defend me for a
                                                    8.
minor traffic violation?

**Clerk:** I _____ _____ said you were arrested. What _____
     9.                                            10.
_____ planning to do? Represent yourself in court?

**Ruggiero:** I don't quite understand _____ _____ mean. And I sure didn't
                                    11.
know _____ _____ can be put in jail for a few unpaid parking
        12.
tickets.

**Clerk:** Oh, just parking tickets? Then I have no idea _____ _____
                                               13.
_____ _____ do. You _____ _____ know if you
14.                          15.
need legal help, _____ _____? You'll _____
            16.                 17.
_____ ask an attorney.

**You may want to read the note of explanation in the appendix.**

**C.** Listen again to Conversation 1 at the beginning of this section (page 54). You may want to circle the phrases that are pronounced as reduced forms. Then, in groups of four, read the conversation aloud.

**D.** *Playing Roles*—Pay special attention to reduced forms as you use the information in this chart to role-play a conversation.

**Role A:** You have a legal problem but don't know if you need to hire a lawyer or not. You want to get your friend's opinion.

**Role B:** You ask your friend questions to figure out if he or she needs to hire a lawyer or not.

### Do You Need an Attorney?

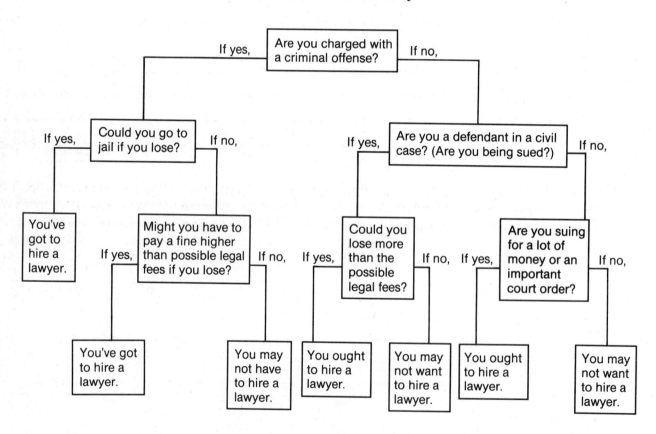

**\*E.** Beyond the text: From books or friends who know something about the law, try to find out more about when a lawyer is necessary. Tell the class what you have learned.

# PART THREE / PRACTICAL LISTENING

● Understanding How Small Claims Courts Function

> Most states have established a system of "small claims" courts or divisions for minor cases that involve amounts of money under a certain limit. You can file a civil (noncriminal) complaint in these lower courts. They don't usually allow lawyers to represent either the plaintiff (the person who is filing the claim) or the defendant (the accused person in the lawsuit) at the hearing.

 **A.** **Read the sentences. Then listen to the hearing in small claims court and write _T_ (true) or _F_ (false) on the lines. Change the false statements to make them correct.**

1. _F_ The insurance claims adjuster, Lester Bucks, is suing the car owner for damage to his firm. *The car owner, Benjamin Stolz, is suing Alexander Smart for damage to his car.*

2. _____ The car owner has filed a claim for a smaller amount than he really feels he should get. _____

3. _____ The accident occurred when one car was legally parked, and there has been no argument over who was at fault. _____

4. _____ Damage to the car was minor, but Mr. Stolz wants compensation for pain and suffering as well. _____

5. _____ The insurance company has agreed to pay the full amount of the average estimate for repairs. _____

6. _____ The owner of the car had been taking excellent care of it before the accident. _____
_____
_____

> In any disagreement or civil case, the judge considers the facts and the evidence presented by both sides. A verdict (a legal judgment) is based on existing laws and precedents (verdicts in similar cases in the past).

 **B.**  **Listen to the court hearing again. Then answer these questions.**

1. What pieces of evidence have the plaintiff (the car owner) and the defendant's representative (the insurance claims adjuster) shown the judge?

   The plaintiff: _____

   The defendant's representative: _____

2. How much is the average estimate for repairs to Mr. Stolz's car? _____ The offer

   of the insurance company? _____

3. How did the insurance claims adjuster arrive at the amount of his company's offer? ____

   _____

4. In your opinion, what is the most important issue to be decided in the case? (Circle the letter.)
   a. Was the defendant totally at fault in the accident?
   b. Does an automobile rise in value if the owner takes very good care of it?
   c. Are the estimates for car repairs and the current market value of the car accurate?
   d. Should the insurance firm pay more for repairs than the current selling price of that make, model, and year of car?
   e. other (a *yes/no* question of your own): _____

   _____

5. Is the answer to the question you circled above *yes* or *no*? ____

6. Who should win the case? _____ Why? _____

   _____

7. If you ruled in favor of the plaintiff, how much money should he receive? _____

   Why? _____

   **(You may want to read the decision in a similar case in the appendix.)**

_____ **\*C.**  **Beyond the text: Videotape or tape record a real or simulated court case from a T.V. or radio program. Begin playing the tape for the class. After the plaintiff and the defendant present their cases, stop the tape and let the other students summarize the evidence and predict the judge's decision. Then play the rest of the tape with the judge's verdict.**

# PART FOUR / LANGUAGE ACTIVITIES

● Understanding Legal Thinking

## A. To role-play small claims court cases in class, follow these steps:

1. Choose a judge and several advisors and a court clerk. Divide the rest of the class into groups of four to six students each.
2. Each group chooses one of the following cases to present or uses a real or imaginary case of its own. Students choose roles—one is the plaintiff, another the defendant, and the others witnesses on either side.
3. Divide your group into two (the plaintiff's and the defendant's sides). In these smaller groups, prepare your case. Collect (or produce) evidence and decide what each person will say in "court."
4. In turn, the court clerk calls each group to present their case before the judge.
5. For each case, the judge asks the plaintiff to tell his or her side of the story first. The judge may choose to just listen and take notes or may help the plaintiff to get to the point quickly by asking questions. The plaintiff's witnesses then add their stories.
6. The defendant then presents his or her side, along with a witness or witnesses. The judge may or may not ask questions.
7. When the judge has heard all of the information, he or she leaves the room with the advisors to reach a verdict.
8. While the judge and the advisors are discussing the case, the class can ask the plaintiff, the defendant, and the witnesses more questions. Then each listener makes his or her own decision and writes it down with the reasons for it.
9. The judge and his or her advisors return to give their verdict and explain their reasoning. Those in the class who agree tell their reasons, and those who disagree explain why.

**(Any decision the judge or students reach may be "correct" for the situation as it was presented in class. For real verdicts in similar cases that came to court, see the appendix.)**

## Case 1: A Disagreement over Car Insurance Reimbursement

THE PLAINTIFF: Before the disagreement arose, you had purchased and paid for full insurance coverage on your new automobile, with only a $50 deductible for collision. (You must pay for the first $50 of damage if an accident is your fault, and the company will pay the rest.) You had also damaged the rear bumper and the trunk of your new car by backing into a post because you'd thought you were in first gear when you were in reverse. The lowest of the two estimates you'd received for repairs was $515, but you'd decided to bring the car to the dealer for repair even though he had given you a much higher estimate. You are suing for the full cost of the dealer's repairs plus court costs.

THE WITNESSES: You are members of the plaintiff's family who also drive the car. You'd been feeling very bad about the damage to the expensive new automobile and had urged the plaintiff to take it to the dealer to make sure it would be repaired properly with new parts.

THE EVIDENCE: a picture of the new car and photos of the damage
a dated purchase agreement with the dealer for the new automobile
a receipt for $925 of car repairs from the dealer

*******

THE DEFENDANT: You are the claims adjuster for the company that is insuring the plaintiff's new car. After the accident, you'd told the defendant to take the car to a repair shop twenty miles away that would replace the damaged parts with used ones for a low price. Your company is only willing to pay $795, the average of the two repair estimates received minus the deductible.

THE WITNESSES: You are representatives of the same insurance firm. You believe that used parts are just as good as new ones and that repairs should be done as cheaply as possible to keep insurance costs down.

THE EVIDENCE: a copy of the plaintiff's insurance policy, which indicates that replacement of parts is covered

## Case 2: A Disagreement over Fees for Service

THE PLAINTIFF: As a dentist, you made a set of upper dentures for the defendant. You'd seen the dental insurance policy that was supposed to cover your fees before you started work, and you'd agreed to accept the insurance payments as compensation in full. You completed the work about six months ago, but you haven't received any money for it yet nor has the defendant come back to your office since that time. You are suing for the reasonable value of your services—$1100.

THE WITNESSES: You are receptionists or dental assistants at the plaintiff's office. You assisted in the work the dentist did for the defendant, who had promised to fill out and send in the claim form to the insurance company right away. But when you called the company to ask about payment, you learned that it had never received the form. The defendant made an appointment about five months ago to see the dentist again but never showed up. Since then you have tried to call the defendant and have sent out several bills and letters but have received no response.

THE EVIDENCE: the signed agreement for work to be done
records of the work completed
a copy of the dentist's fee schedule
copies of the bills and letters sent to the defendant

THE DEFENDANT: You hadn't been to a dentist in many years because you were afraid of the pain and the dentist's bills. Finally, when your firm added a complete dental plan to its employee benefits package, you made an appointment. Your teeth were in terrible condition by that time. The dentist did a lot of work, pulled most of your top teeth, and made you a set of upper dentures. You had lost your insurance form and couldn't send it in, and after two weeks you called the dentist to make another appointment because the dentures didn't fit correctly. But you didn't show up for the appointment because you didn't trust the dentist's work and didn't want to pay extra money. At the hearing, you are planning to give the dentures back to the dentist.

THE WITNESSES: You are members of the defendant's family. You don't know much about the health insurance system in this country because you are newcomers. You know that the defendant has been having a lot of pain and hasn't been able to wear the dentures.

THE EVIDENCE: a set of upper dentures that don't fit well

## Case 3: A Disagreement over Work Performed

THE PLAINTIFF: You are the owner of a burglar alarm company. The defendant had signed an agreement to buy a $980 system from you and had paid half that amount in advance but had refused to pay the rest upon completion of the work. You are suing for an additional $490 plus court costs.

THE WITNESSES: You are electricians (employees of the plaintiff). You installed the burglar alarm system in the defendant's store. It had an automatic dialer that you were supposed to connect to the store's phone line so that if anyone broke in, the alarm would notify the police. But because you couldn't find the appropriate wires, you hooked up the system to the public pay phone instead.

THE EVIDENCE: the written agreement for the purchase of the system

\*\*\*\*\*\*

THE DEFENDANT: You are the owner of a doughnut shop that had had frequent burglaries. Finally you signed an agreement to purchase a burglar alarm system and paid half the total cost at that time. When you opened the store three days after the electricians had installed the system, you found that burglars had broken in, stolen money, and destroyed one of the machines. The alarm hadn't functioned as promised to notify the police, so you refused to pay the rest of the bill.

THE WITNESSES: You are self-employed electricians the defendant contacted after the burglar alarm system in the store failed to operate as expected. You figured out that in order for it to work correctly, the burglars would have had to put money into the public pay phone it was connected to. You rewired the system for a fee of $55.

EVIDENCE: an expert's written estimate of the loss and the damage from the burglary ($1380)

\*B. **Beyond the text: Visit the small claims division of your local court on a day when court is in session. Observe the procedure carefully and take notes. Then, in class, tell your opinions about the cases and the decisions.**

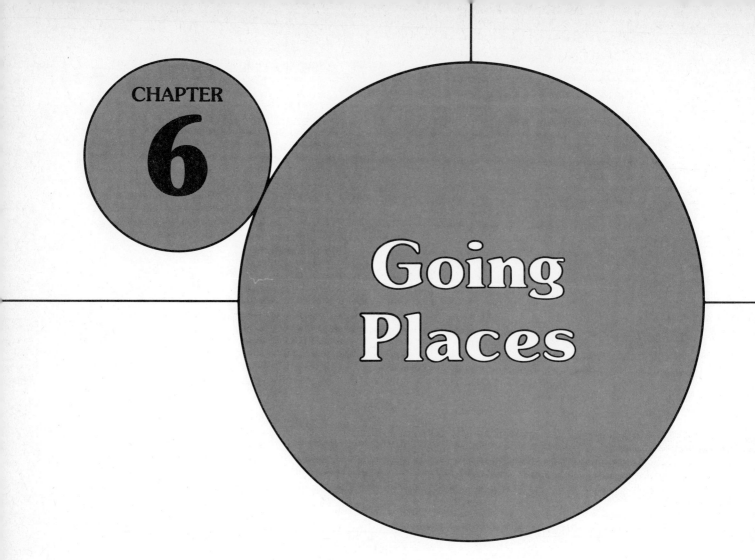

CHAPTER

**6**

# Going Places

**COMPETENCIES:**  Recognizing common travel problems
Recognizing advice
Requesting and giving travel advice
Gathering and using travel information
Planning a vacation

**PRONUNCIATION:**  Recognizing sound linking

**GRAMMAR FOCUS:**  Modal verbs

# PART ONE / LEARNING TO LISTEN

● Recognizing Common Travel Problems ● Recognizing Advice

## Vocabulary and Prelistening

___

**A.** **Read the words and phrases. (You may want to pronounce them and discuss the meanings.)**

| Nouns | | Adjectives | Expressions/Idioms |
|---|---|---|---|
| travelers | itinerary | minor | run into |
| cruise | guide | experienced | miss the boat |
| islands | strike | major | from coast to coast |
| sailing | airline | romantic | unlimited mileage passes |
| dock | | scheduled | tourist attractions |
| refund | **Verbs** | extra | interstate highways |
| fare | avoid | crowded | travel agent |
| route | allow | monotonous | full price |
| sightseeing | suggest | tasty | in advance |
| scenery | advise | uncomfortable | escorted tour |
| passengers | refund | relaxing | to tell you the truth |
| vacation | | reserved | a long time to come |

**What do you think is happening in the pictures? To prepare to listen, make up a story about them with some of the above vocabulary.**

**B.** *Getting the Main Ideas*—Listen to the story, "Travel Mistakes." Then circle the letter of the one correct ending for each sentence.

1. Experienced travelers who know what to expect shouldn't _____.
   a. take a romantic cruise
   b. travel by train
   c. have major difficulties or trouble

2. The kinds of travel discussed in the story are train and bus trips, _____.
   a. cruises, and escorted tours
   b. rental car arrangements, and private touring
   c. bicycle tours, and home-stay itineraries

3. The couple in the story _____.
   a. have enjoyed their last three vacations very much
   b. would rather stay in one place (a four-star hotel) than cover long distances
   c. need a way to avoid problems in their future travels

---

### Recognizing Advice

The main purpose of stories about difficulties and problems may be to give listeners implied advice.

---

**C.** Read these sentence beginnings. Then listen to the story again and complete these suggestions and recommendations by writing the important words on the lines.

1. Because long-distance trains are often many hours late, you might need to take

_____ to _____.

2. If you're taking a cruise, be sure to arrive at the dock on time because there won't

be _____.

3. If you miss the boat, you may have to pay for _____.

4. To save money on bus travel if you want to cover a lot of miles, you can buy _____

_____.

5. To see as many places as possible and not have to pay for hotels, you might decide to

_____, but it may be impossible to _____.

6. It might not be a good idea to take a very long bus trip because the scenery _____

_____, the food _____, the restrooms

_____, and it may be difficult to _____

_____ and the other passengers _____.

7. If you pay for an escorted tour in advance, the travel agency may not be able to

_____ unless _____.

**\*D.** In one sentence each, summarize each of the three travel experiences from the story. (You can look back at the pictures, if necessary.) Try to explain the point of the story. (Then you may want to read the note of explanation in the appendix.)

**E.** *Telling Your Story*—In small groups, describe a travel experience that you have had. If you had difficulties, ask other students to give you advice on how to avoid those kinds of problems in the future.

# PART TWO / PRONUNCIATION THROUGH ROLE-PLAY

● Requesting and Giving Travel Advice  ● Recognizing Sound Linking

 **A.**  **Listen to this conversation.**

**Traveler:** Could you please give me information on air fares from Miami to Bellingham, Washington? We'd like advice on how to fly as cheaply as possible.

**Travel agent:** Let's see . . . I wouldn't advise you to pay the normal one-way coach fare of $555. If you can fly on a Tuesday or Wednesday and buy your tickets at least twenty-one days in advance, I'd suggest you book a round-trip excursion flight.

**Traveler:** But we may not need the return tickets.

**Agent:** That's all right. Even if you don't use them, you should be able to save $89 over the one-way fare. Of course, I'd recommend early booking. You ought to try to reserve the "Super Saver" seats. There are only a few of them, and they're fifteen percent cheaper than the others.

**Traveler:** That sounds like a good idea.

**Agent:** Wait . . . to save another $100 or so, why don't you book a flight to Vancouver, Canada?

**Traveler:** But that's farther than we want to go.

**Agent:** I know. But you can take a bus from Vancouver back to Bellingham and still save money. And if you're traveling with children, you might be able to get a discount if you fly economy class but they don't. But to take advantage of the airlines' guaranteed fare policy, you'd have to make reservations and pay for your tickets at least six weeks in advance. Shall I begin the search for available seats?

**Traveler:** No, thank you.

**Agent:** Excuse me?

**Traveler:** I may call you back . . . if we don't decide to drive.

**Summarize what happened in your own words. Try to explain the point of the story. (Then you may want to read the note of explanation in the appendix.)**

In spoken English, there are few clear sound separations between words. Within a thought group, sounds are linked together so that a phrase may sound like one long word:

1. You can link a vowel sound at the end of a word to a vowel sound at the beginning of the next word, sometimes with the addition of a slight "y" or "w" sound ( ⌣ = sound linking).

**Examples:**

be(y)a problem      be(y)able to      go(w)on      two(w)hours

2. You can link a consonant sound at the end of a word to a vowel sound at the beginning of the next word. (The "h" sound may seem to disappear at the beginning of an unstressed syllable.)

**Examples:**

That's a good idea. = "That-sa-goo-di-dea"
Ask him for his advice. = "As-kim-for-i-zad-vice"
might have tried a little = "mi-tuv-trie-da-little"

3. You can link a sound at the end of a word to a sound at the beginning of the next word that is pronounced the same or similarly.

**Examples:**

know what to expect      a romantic cruise      like good tickets

**B.**   **Listen to these examples of sound linking. A curved line ( ⌣ ) indicates sound linking, and a line ( ╱ ) through the letter _h_ indicates it is not pronounced.**

**Traveler:** I'd like information on air fares to Oklahoma City.

**Agent:** Certainly. Round trip or one way?

**Traveler:** Round trip in coach or economy class, please.

**Agent:** That fare is six sixty eight.

**Traveler:** Six hundred sixty-eight dollars? That must be the full fare. My friend has

called a travel agent too, and he told him he could get a discount rate

for himself and his wife.

**Agent:** To fly at the lowest price, you must travel late at night, leave on a Tuesday or

Wednesday, stay one Sunday, and pay at least seven days in advance.

But those seats are limited.

**C.**   **Listen again to the conversation at the beginning of this section (page 65). You may want to draw a curved line for clear examples of sound linking. Then, in pairs, read the conversation aloud.**

**D.** *Playing Roles*—Pay special attention to sound linking as you complete these activities.

1. In pairs, have the following conversation. The first student begins with the first sentence on the left. The second student chooses and responds with the most appropriate sentences on the right, the first student continues with the most appropriate sentences on the left, and so on. To make the activity more difficult, you might want to cover the side of the page that your partner is using.

| EXAMPLES: | Student A | Student B |
|---|---|---|
| | Could you please give me some information on low-cost Caribbean cruises for my parents? | Low-cost? I'd recommend one of our special spring break cruises out of Miami. |

| Student A | Student B |
|---|---|
| Could you please give me some information on low-cost Caribbean cruises for my parents? | They don't have to go with students. They could take the same cruise one or two weeks before school lets out. How about the second or third week of March? |
| But they'd like to stop as often as possible to go shopping; they're bargain hunters. | Yes, some discounts are good year round, but off-season rates may be even lower. And to save even more money, I'd advise them to take a cruise that doesn't stop in many ports. |
| But aren't your low-price travel rates for senior citizens good all year round? | Low-cost? I'd recommend one of our special spring break cruises out of Miami. |
| But won't it be cool in March? Do you think they ought to be traveling so early in the year? | Yes, I do. They'll enjoy the cool, clear weather; the ship won't be so crowded and the prices should be lower. |
| Spring break? But they're in their sixties. Are you suggesting they travel with hundreds of college students? | Yes, I recommend them very highly. If I were you, I'd book right away. And it might be a good idea to arrange an air-sea package. |
| That three-day cruise sounds interesting. Would you recommend the food and the entertainment? | Why don't you read this about three-day shopping cruises in this brochure from the Tropical Seas Line? |
| But they don't need to fly to the dock. They live in Miami. | |

2. Tell some phrases you could use to request or give travel advice or suggestions. Your instructor will list them on the board. **Examples:**

Could you suggest...?
I'd recommend (that)....
To..., you could + VERB....

What would you advise me to do?
It might be a good idea to + VERB....
Why don't you + VERB...?

3. In groups of four or more, ask for and make travel suggestions. Three students in each group play the roles of travel agents who know about one of the following kinds of information. The fourth plays the role of a traveler who wants advice. **Examples:**

**Traveler 1:** Would you recommend that I travel by air or by train?

**Agent 1:** If you're in a hurry, I advise you to take a plane.

**Agent 2:** But if you'd like to relax and see the scenery, why don't you consider train travel?

**Agent 3:** You should drive. I suggest that we plan your itinerary first. Then we can look into car rentals.

**Traveler 2:** But I'd rather not be responsible for a car, and I'd heard we could get a discount on hotels if we flew.

## Air Travel

- fastest way to travel
- nonstop flights best / direct flights stop in one or two places / connecting flights— must change planes
- types of airplanes: jumbo jets (two aisles and more room) / 747s and L-1011s (320–370 seats in different arrangements) / smaller planes for short flights
- snacks, meals, entertainment good for children / may be conveniences and special food for babies
- no-frills flight: lowest cost possible
- charter flights: low cost / payment well in advance / restrictions / penalties for cancellation / may not keep schedules / may be cancelled
- tour packages: combine air travel with hotel accommodations

## Train (Amtrak or Canadian National Railways)

- train stations more convenient than airport?
- relaxing / comfortable / can read, sleep, meet people
- family plan / discount children's fare / special promotional fares
- national train timetable from Amtrak offices (routes and schedules)
- car rental and tour packages available
- different features on different trains: snack bar or dining car / sleeping accommodations / checking baggage through to destination

## Renting a Car

- get information from local automobile club, tourist office, yellow pages of telephone book, or travel ads
- smaller, local companies cheaper / rent older cars for less
- size and kind of car? (comfort, room for children to play, etc.)
- features of car? (amount of room, tape deck, automatic transmission, air conditioning, etc.)
- cost: mileage charges additional? extra fees? taxes and insurance included?
- weekend or low-season charges lower than midweek or high season
- make reservations well ahead of time / get confirmation in writing
- keep rental agency's service phone number with you
- check that you can work everything on car and that agency has made note of all previous damage

**\*E.**   **Beyond the Text: At a local travel agency, get brochures, schedules, or other information that interests you. If a travel agent is not busy, you might ask for information, but be sure to tell him or her if you are not planning a trip at this time. Use the information you have collected for more role-playing or exchange of advice with your classmates.**

# PART THREE / PRACTICAL LISTENING

● Gathering and Using Travel Information

There are many different ways to travel. Those who like to travel with comfort may choose to pay high prices for luxury even if they must save for a long time to be able to afford a trip. Those who prefer to economize will probably shop around for travel bargains. Some travelers plan to be busy every minute so that they don't miss any sights or experiences, while others hate to plan ahead because they'd rather take it easy and leave plenty of time for relaxation. Still others may prefer to pass up the popular tourist attractions in order to meet people and to learn about everyday life in new places.

 **A.** **Listen to Stories 1–3 and match them with the pictures by writing 1–3 in the boxes. Tell the "clues" from which you inferred your answers.**

**B.** **Listen to Story 1 again. Then circle the letter of the item in each pair that is probably more expensive.**

1. a. first-class air travel
   b. an excursion fare in coach

2. a. renting a new car
   b. driving your own car

3. a. a bed-and-breakfast inn
   b. a four-star hotel

4. a. hotel room service
   b. breakfast in a coffee shop

5. a. a cafeteria
   b. a restaurant where you must make reservations

6. a. tourist attraction fees
   b. hiring a private guide

**C.** **Listen to Story 2 again. Then match each source of travel information with a reason for using it by writing the letters a–e on the lines.**

1. _C_ a novel or historical account

2. ____ tourist boards, chambers of commerce, etc.

3. ____ the *Readers' Guide* at the library

4. ____ advertising in local newspapers

5. ____ travel guidebooks

a. to get free maps, brochures, posters, newsletters, etc.

b. to learn about sightseeing, accommodations, and restaurants

c. to get a feeling for a place

d. to find out about popular places and travel bargains

e. to locate articles in past magazines and newspapers

**D.** **Listen to Story 3 again. Then write the names of the organizations or programs that the travelers might contact in each situation. (You may want to look up the addresses of these organizations in the appendix and write them for information.)**

1. We'd like to exchange apartments with a family in another country for the summer:
   *International Home Exchange Service*

2. We'll be taking trains from place to place and would like low-cost, friendly accommodations with other travelers: _____

3. We could see the scenery by bicycle: _____

4. We might go to Ontario or Quebec, and we'd like to share in family life there: _____

5. We believe in peace and international friendship, and it might be interesting to meet people in their homes: _____

6. My parents could continue their education during their travels: _____

**\*E.** **Beyond the text: In small groups, discuss your answers to these questions:**

1. How do you like to travel? Give examples.
2. Where would you prefer to get travel information? Why?
3. Do you know about any travel organizations? Tell what they offer, what they require of members, etc.

# PART FOUR / LANGUAGE ACTIVITIES

● Planning a Vacation

> To avoid unnecessary difficulties and to make sure you have a good time, it's a good idea to plan vacation trips in advance. You ought to consider the reasons you will be traveling, the activities you can enjoy in the amount of time you have, the amount of money you can spend, and so on.

**A.** **Which of these possible reasons for travel are important to you? Check one, two, or three of them. Then tell a partner your answers and the reasons for them.**

1. _____ to get away from everyday worries and to rest and relax
2. _____ to be physically active and perhaps have adventures
3. _____ to be entertained
4. _____ to have educational or cultural experiences
5. _____ to have contact with people
6. _____ to experience luxury (a high degree of comfort)

**B.** **For the purposes you checked in Exercise A, rate these possible travel activities in order. Write 1 on the line before the activity that would be most enjoyable for you, 2 before the next most attractive activity, and so on.**

1. _____ being passive: sunbathing, watching T.V., sleeping, doing nothing, etc.
2. _____ participating in sports: tennis, soccer, running, bowling, etc.
3. _____ exploring nature: hiking, mountain climbing, rafting, horseback riding, camping, etc.
4. _____ enjoying entertainment: shows, plays, movies, concerts, etc.
5. _____ experiencing culture: museums, historical sites, etc.
6. _____ visiting tourist attractions: amusement parks, famous sites, etc.
7. _____ exploring unusual places: a jungle, a river, the wilderness, a village, etc.
8. _____ getting to know travel companions better and making contact: meeting people, making new friends
9. _____ having comfortable accommodations: a hotel, a resort, a lodge, etc.
10. _____ eating: having elegant restaurant meals, trying new kinds of food, etc.

**C.** **In pairs, try to agree on six activities that you would like to participate in during a vacation and list them in order of importance here. If you can't come to any agreement or compromise, change partners.**

1. _____     4. _____
2. _____     5. _____
3. _____     6. _____

_____ **D.** With your partner, choose one of these kinds of places to visit together on a three-day trip. Make sure that you will be able to enjoy all or most of the activities there that you listed in Exercise C. Write the name of a specific place on the line. (If you can't come to any agreement or compromise, change partners.)

1. a big city (Which one?) _____

2. a national or state park (Which one?) _____

3. the mountains (Where?) _____

4. the seashore (Where?) _____

5. a resort (What kind and where?) _____

6. other (What and where?) _____

_____ **E.** Join another pair of students and tell them the place you chose in Exercise D. Decide on a place that all four students would like to visit (the suggestion of one of the pairs or a third place). Write it here and tell it to the class. (If you can't come to any agreement or compromise, join a different pair or group of four students.)

_____

_____ **\*F.** Beyond the text: From your school or public library, a tourist bureau, a chamber of commerce, a travel agency, etc., get information (guidebooks, maps, brochures, newsletters, etc.) about the place you chose. Then, in your group of two to six students, make travel decisions for a three-day trip by agreeing on answers to these questions. Write your answers here or on a piece of paper. (Come to an agreement or compromise; don't change groups at this point.) Then summarize your decisions for the class.

1. transportation: How will you get there? _____

2. accommodations: Where will you stay? _____

3. meals: When and where will you eat? _____

_____

4. activities: What will you do? _____

_____

5. itinerary: What is your daily plan?

Day 1: _____

_____

Day 2: _____

_____

Day 3: _____

_____

6. price: How much will this trip cost each of you? _____

7. luggage: What kinds of things will you bring along? _____

How much can each traveler bring? _____

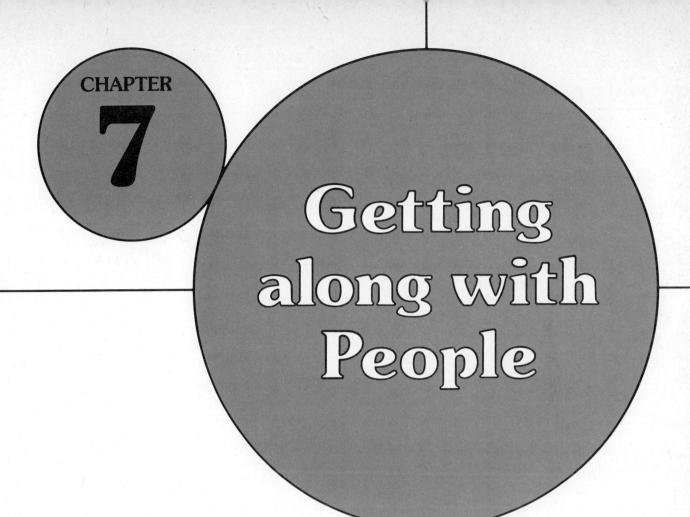

**CHAPTER**

# 7

# Getting along with People

**COMPETENCIES:** Recognizing traditional and changing sex roles
Recognizing examples that support a point of view
Recognizing stereotypes
Understanding various kinds of personal relationships
Filling out a compatibility questionnaire

**PRONUNCIATION:** Recognizing stressed content words

**GRAMMAR FOCUS:** Adjectives and adverbs
Comparative and superlative forms

# PART ONE / LEARNING TO LISTEN

● Recognizing Traditional and Changing Sex Roles ● Recognizing Examples That Support a Point of View

## Vocabulary and Prelistening

**A.** Read the words and phrases. (You may want to pronounce them and discuss the meanings.)

| Nouns | | Adjectives/Adverbs | Expressions/Idioms |
|---|---|---|---|
| male | colleagues | traditional | fulfill roles |
| female | career | exclusively | fields of work |
| stereotypes | receptionist | creative | speak up |
| homemakers | welder | charming | construction site |
| responsibility | | irritated | matter-of-fact |
| salaries | | ridiculous | mow the lawn |

To prepare to listen, answer these questions about the pictures with some of the above vocabulary: What kind of work is each person doing? Is this a traditional job for a male or a female? Why?

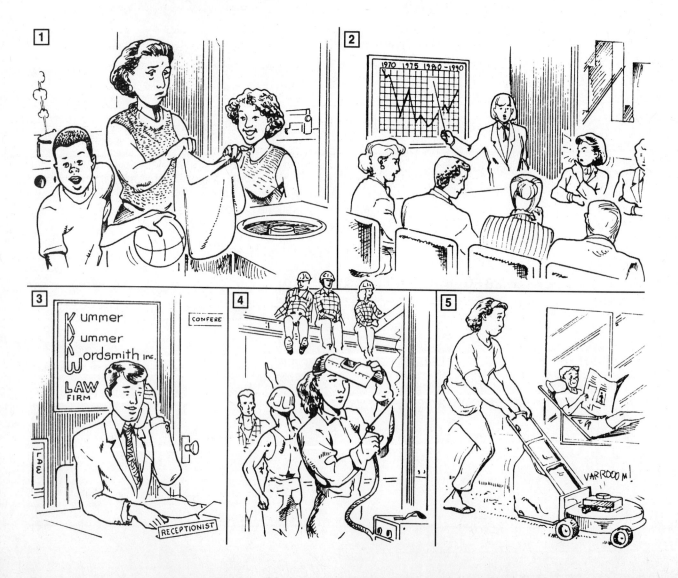

**B.**   *Getting the Main Ideas*—Listen to the story, "Changing Roles." Then circle the letter of the one correct ending for each sentence.

1. In the past, some kinds of work have been considered traditionally men's, like _____.
   a. being a homemaker
   b. welding and mowing lawns
   c. being a receptionist in a law office

2. Male and female roles in the world of work _____.
   a. have changed so much that women generally earn higher salaries than men do now
   b. haven't changed as much in the past twenty years as in the previous century
   c. are changing more quickly now than ever before

---

### Recognizing Examples That Support a Point of View

To support their point of view (opinions), most speakers give specific examples, perhaps from personal experience.

---

 **C.**   Listen to the story again and pay special attention to the examples that support the speaker's main ideas. Complete these illustrations of her statements by writing the important words on the lines.

1. In business, there seem to be fewer and fewer differences between the sexes: at office meetings and in group discussions, women might _____, _____, and _____ than their male colleagues.

2. The old stereotypes of men's and women's work have been changing: my daughter is going out on a date with a _____ and has gotten a job as a _____.

3. Maybe my husband's views of sex roles aren't so outdated after all: he got me to _____.

**\*D.**   In as few sentences as possible, summarize the examples that the speaker has given. (You can look back at the last four pictures, if necessary.) Try to explain the point of the story. (Then you may want to read the note of explanation in the appendix.)

_____ **E.** *Telling Your Story*—In small groups, name the kinds of work that you believe have been considered traditionally "men's work" and "women's work" in this culture in the past (Examples: "Men's work": construction work, busing tables in restaurants; "Women's work": elementary school teaching, secretarial work). Try to agree on the six "most traditional" jobs for each and write them in these lists.

"Men's Work"

1. _____
2. _____
3. _____
4. _____
5. _____
6. _____

"Women's Work"

1. _____
2. _____
3. _____
4. _____
5. _____
6. _____

As the kinds of work the groups agreed on are read aloud, your instructor will list them on the chalkboard, tallying ( ///// // ) with marks those that more than one group has mentioned. When all of the groups have contributed, he or she will circle the jobs with the most tally marks. Then, in your groups, discuss your answers to these questions:

1. Why are the circled jobs traditionally considered the field of one sex more than the other? Do you think these reasons are valid or logical? Why or why not?
2. Do you believe the fields the circled jobs represent have been changing? If so, how? If not, why not?
3. Would you like to work in a field considered "nontraditional" for people of your sex? If so, which one and why? If not, why not?

_____ ***F.** Beyond the text: Do you know anyone who has been doing a kind of work considered "nontraditional" for people of that sex? If so, ask him or her questions about the work and summarize what you have learned for the class. (If possible, invite him or her to speak to the class about his or her experiences on the job.)

# PART TWO / PRONUNCIATION THROUGH ROLE-PLAY

● Recognizing Stereotypes ● Recognizing Stressed Content Words

 **A.** **Listen to these thoughts.**

**Summarize what happened in your own words. Try to explain the point of the story. (Then you may want to read the note of explanation in the appendix.)**

In general, in spoken English, the content words of a sentence (those that carry the meaning) are usually stressed, while the function words are usually unstressed.

| Content Words | Examples | Function Words | Examples |
|---|---|---|---|
| nouns | women, man, feelings | articles | a, an, the |
| main verbs (except *be*) | listen, say, understand | personal pronouns | he, him, them, we, I |
| adjectives | boring, worst, emotional | prepositions | in, at, to, as, for |
| adverbs | quickly, too, often | conjunctions | and, but, so, as |

 **B.**    **Listen to this conversation. The underlined words are stressed.**

**Husband:** It's the most <u>beautiful</u> <u>night</u> we've had in a <u>long</u> <u>time</u>. The <u>air</u> is <u>clear</u>, it's <u>warm</u> and <u>pleasant</u>, and the <u>stars</u> are <u>bright</u>. I don't <u>suppose</u> you'd be <u>interested</u> in a <u>romantic</u> <u>stroll</u> in the <u>moonlight</u>, would you?

**Wife:** A <u>romantic</u> <u>stroll</u>? <u>Yeah</u> . . . why <u>not</u>? <u>Bye</u>. I'll be <u>back</u> in <u>about</u> an <u>hour</u>.

 **C.**    **Listen to this conversation and underline the content words that are stressed.**

**Husband:** <u>Women!</u> I don't <u>understand</u> them. They're so much more emotional than men.

**Wife:** And I'll never understand men. I know they have feelings, but they rarely express them.

**Husband:** Women are always trying to get what they want with tears. If they thought as logically and reasonably as men, couples would have better relationships.

**Wife:** Men are insensitive. All a woman wants is some attention, an occasional gift—perhaps flowers—and a little romance.

**Husband:** Do you really believe in those male-female stereotypes?

**Wife:** No.

**Husband:** Then let's stop this ridiculous argument and go for a romantic walk in the moonlight.

 **D.**    **Listen again to the thoughts at the beginning of this section (page 77). You may want to underline the content words that are stressed. Then, in pairs, read the thoughts aloud.**

## E.    *Playing Roles*—Pay special attention to stressed content words and unstressed function words as you complete these activities.

1.  If possible, divide the class into two same-sex groups (one men and the other women). (If there are many more men than women or vice versa, divide into two equal groups of students.)

2.  With your group, discuss and list stereotypical generalizations that members of your sex might make about members of the opposite sex. **Examples:**

    Men...                                Women...
    ...are aggressive and competitive.    ...get too emotional.
    ...try too hard to win at sports.     ...don't think logically.

3.  In turn, each member of the women's group makes a different comment about men in general. The men's group listens and may take notes, but shouldn't say anything.

4.  In turn, each member of the men's group makes a different comment about women in general. The women listen and may take notes but shouldn't say anything.

5.  Without getting overly emotional or arguing, tell your opinions of some of the other group's comments about members of your sex. Which do you agree with in general, and why? Which do you disagree with in general, and why? (Remember that there are always many exceptions to any generalization.)

6.  Tell your opinions of stereotypical generalizations. Are they ever useful? Why or why not?

# PART THREE / PRACTICAL LISTENING

● Understanding Various Kinds of Personal Relationships

 **A.** **Listen to Conversations 1–4 and match them with the pictures by writing the numbers 1–4 in the boxes. Tell the "clues" from which you inferred your answers.**

**B.** Read these sentences. Then listen to each conversation again and circle the letters of the two inferences you can make from it. (Don't circle the letters of the other statements even if you think they are true.) Tell the reasons for your answers.

## Conversation 1

a. Joe is dating more than one woman during the same period of time.
b. He's as honest with all of them as he can be so that they don't have any unrealistic expectations of him.
c. He hasn't told each of his girlfriends about any of the others.
d. Tony thinks Joe is treating his female friends much worse than he would in the same situation.

## Conversation 2

a. David and Harold have quite different life styles because one is married with children and the other is unmarried.
b. Married life is much lonelier than single life because husbands and wives don't get involved in useful projects.
c. Because most single men and women lead exciting social lives, they rarely feel depressed or alone.
d. Harold complains, but he'd really rather be single than married at the present time.

## Conversation 3

a. Cindy likes Steve more than Lisa does, but she's afraid to talk to him because Lisa is so jealous.
b. Lisa doesn't want Steve to know she's interested in him because she's trying to be "cool."
c. Steve might have wanted to join Cindy and Lisa's conversation, but they didn't seem to have noticed him, so he didn't.
d. In personal or social situations, young people (and older ones too) usually say exactly what they mean and clearly show how they feel about one another.

## Conversation 4

a. Martin and Sally have been having an argument about the stereo system.
b. He's feeling romantic, but she isn't.
c. Martin and Sally have been going out together, but they probably don't know each other very well yet.
d. It may be difficult for one person in a relationship to express his or her feelings first, and it could be embarrassing.

**\*C.** Look again at the pictures at the beginning of this section. Then answer these questions about each situation:

1. What kind of relationship do the people have (casual, friendly, supportive, honest, etc.)? Do they communicate well? Why or why not?
2. Do you think they should do or say anything to improve their relationship? If not, why not? If so, what?

# PART FOUR / LANGUAGE ACTIVITIES

● Filling Out a Compatibility Questionnaire

> Whether they are looking for husbands or wives, roommates, or friends to
> share interests with, many people are concerned about compatibility—the
> ability to get along well together. Single people who join computer dating
> services may fill out "compatibility questionnaires" that ask about their
> personal characteristics, beliefs, and interests.

**A.** **To fill out the compatability questionnaire on the next two pages, check one box for your answer to each question unless the instructions indicate that you can check as many as apply. If none of the answers exactly fits you, check the closest one. You may want to make a copy of the questionnaire before you fill it out so that you don't have to tear it out of your book for Step 2. Then, follow these steps:**

1. Your instructor will give each student a card or a slip of paper with a different number on it. Write your name on the card or slip and write the number on your questionnaire. Do not write your name on your questionnaire.

2. Your instructor will collect the cards or slips of paper and put them aside. He or she will then collect the questionnaires, mix them up, and pass them around the room for everyone to read. When you have finished looking at each one and have decided if you are interested in that person, pass the questionnaire to the student on your right. (You should be reading only one questionnaire at a time so that everyone in the class has one to look at.)

3. When you read the questionnaire of someone you'd like to get to know better, write its number on a piece of paper before you pass on the questionnaire. Be selective—write down only the numbers of those people who you think you'd be especially compatible with. When you have read all of the questionnaires, give your list of numbers, with your name on the list, to your instructor. He or she will add the names of all the students whose numbers you have chosen and return your list to you.

4. In or out of class, get together with one of the students on your list and have a conversation about your beliefs and interests. Then tell the class your answers to these questions: Do you think you are compatible (able to get along well)? If not, why not? If yes, for what purpose (dating, friendship, sharing activities, being roommates, etc.)?

5. You may want to repeat Step 4 with one or more other students on your list.

**\*B.** **Beyond the text: In small groups or as a class, answer these questions:**

1. Do you think compatibility questionnaires are useful? If so, for what purpose? If not, why not?

2. In your opinion, what makes two people compatible?

# Compatibility Questionnaire

**1.** Your age:
☐ under 20   ☐ 21-30   ☐ 31-40   ☐ 41-50   ☐ 51-60   ☐ over 60

**2.** Your sex:   ☐ male   ☐ female

**3.** Your religion:   ☐ Catholic   ☐ Protestant   ☐ Jewish
☐ Islamic   ☐ other non-Christian   ☐ none

**4.** How important is religion in your life?
☐ very important   ☐ important   ☐ somewhat important   ☐ not important at all

**5.** Your political beliefs:
☐ liberal   ☐ middle-of-the-road   ☐ conservative   ☐ none

**6.** Your place of birth:
☐ U.S./Canada   ☐ Latin America   ☐ Europe
☐ Asia   ☐ Africa   ☐ other

**7.** What language(s) do you speak? (Check all answers that apply.)
☐ English   ☐ Portuguese   ☐ French   ☐ Japanese   ☐ Farsi
☐ Spanish   ☐ Italian   ☐ German   ☐ Chinese   ☐ other

**8.** How much education have you had?
☐ elementary school   ☐ high school grad   ☐ college grad
☐ some high school   ☐ some college   ☐ graduate degree

**9.** What was your favorite school subject?
☐ math and science   ☐ social sciences   ☐ physical education
☐ literature   ☐ languages   ☐ none

**10.** What kind of work do you do for a living? (Check one or more.)
☐ professional   ☐ artistic/creative   ☐ physical labor
☐ managerial   ☐ white collar/office   ☐ housework
☐ technical   ☐ own business   ☐ other

**11.** Which of these are important to you? (Check all that apply.)
☐ women's issues   ☐ exercise   ☐ money   ☐ power
☐ health foods   ☐ astrology   ☐ family   ☐ none of these

**12.** What minimum income would you consider adequate per person?
☐ under $10,000   ☐ $15,000–$20,000   ☐ $30,000–$45,000
☐ $10,000–$15,000   ☐ $20,000–$30,000   ☐ over $45,000

**13.** Which of these activities do you or would you enjoy? (Check all that apply.)
☐ drawing/painting   ☐ jogging   ☐ eating
☐ playing music   ☐ aerobics   ☐ cooking
☐ card games   ☐ flying   ☐ writing
☐ board games   ☐ bicycling   ☐ studying
☐ fixing things   ☐ swimming   ☐ working
☐ home decorating   ☐ skiing   ☐ entertaining
☐ driving a car   ☐ tennis   ☐ partying
☐ horseback riding   ☐ dancing   ☐ gambling
☐ camping/hiking   ☐ singing   ☐ smoking
☐ watching sports   ☐ acting   ☐ watching T.V.
☐ soccer/football   ☐ talking   ☐ volunteer work
☐ baseball/basketball   ☐ drinking   ☐ traveling

**14.** Where do you like to go when you are with a friend or on a date? (Check all that apply.)

- ☐ sports events
- ☐ outside in nature
- ☐ amusement parks
- ☐ each other's homes
- ☐ concerts
- ☐ plays
- ☐ movies
- ☐ dinner
- ☐ dancing
- ☐ museums
- ☐ trips
- ☐ long walks

**15.** Which of these words describe you? (Check all that apply.)

- ☐ creative
- ☐ intelligent
- ☐ cultured
- ☐ interesting
- ☐ boring
- ☐ talkative
- ☐ funny
- ☐ silly
- ☐ serious
- ☐ responsible
- ☐ good-looking
- ☐ athletic
- ☐ healthy
- ☐ stylish
- ☐ picky
- ☐ neat
- ☐ messy
- ☐ organized
- ☐ impersonal
- ☐ emotional
- ☐ logical
- ☐ practical
- ☐ aggressive
- ☐ competitive
- ☐ sociable
- ☐ honest
- ☐ lonely
- ☐ depressed
- ☐ energetic
- ☐ jealous
- ☐ optimistic
- ☐ old-fashioned
- ☐ well-informed

**16.** Which of these words describe the kinds of people you like to spend the most time with? (Check all that apply.)

- ☐ creative
- ☐ intelligent
- ☐ cultured
- ☐ interesting
- ☐ boring
- ☐ talkative
- ☐ funny
- ☐ silly
- ☐ serious
- ☐ sensitive
- ☐ good-looking
- ☐ punctual
- ☐ athletic
- ☐ healthy
- ☐ stylish
- ☐ picky
- ☐ neat
- ☐ messy
- ☐ organized
- ☐ impersonal
- ☐ emotional
- ☐ logical
- ☐ practical
- ☐ sincere
- ☐ aggressive
- ☐ competitive
- ☐ sociable
- ☐ honest
- ☐ lonely
- ☐ depressed
- ☐ energetic
- ☐ jealous
- ☐ optimistic
- ☐ old-fashioned
- ☐ well-informed
- ☐ exciting

**17.** What kinds of music do you enjoy? (Check all that apply.)

- ☐ classical
- ☐ country/western
- ☐ Latin American
- ☐ show tunes
- ☐ popular
- ☐ religious
- ☐ folk
- ☐ jazz
- ☐ other

**18.** What kinds of T.V. or radio programs do you prefer?

- ☐ news and features
- ☐ movies/plays
- ☐ science fiction
- ☐ police/detective
- ☐ comedies
- ☐ talk shows
- ☐ variety/music
- ☐ soap operas
- ☐ drama
- ☐ game shows
- ☐ sports
- ☐ none

**19.** How often do you read newspapers or magazines?

- ☐ every day
- ☐ several times a week
- ☐ rarely
- ☐ never

**20.** Do you have children?

- ☐ yes (living with me)
- ☐ yes (living elsewhere)
- ☐ no

CHAPTER

**8**

# Having Fun

**COMPETENCIES:**    Expressing interests
Recognizing specialized vocabulary
Expressing, accepting, and turning down invitations
Understanding descriptions of sports events
Understanding and describing the rules of games

**PRONUNCIATION:**    Recognizing stress and pitch patterns in phrases

**GRAMMAR FOCUS:**    Gerunds and verb complements
Phrasal verbs

# PART ONE / LEARNING TO LISTEN

● Expressing Interests ● Recognizing Specialized Vocabulary

## Vocabulary and Prelistening

**A.** **Read the words and phrases. (You may want to pronounce them and discuss the meanings.)**

| Nouns | Verbs | Adjectives/Adverbs | Expressions/Idioms |
|---|---|---|---|
| culture | appreciate | single | classical music |
| literature | fidget | particularly | adventure and horror films |
| theater | attend | unanimous | have in mind |
| concert | interrupt | apologetically | shot attempts |
| performance | protest | foreign | change the channel |
| plays | throw | classic | rock music |
| novel | kick | enthusiastically | full volume |
| | argue | excitedly | can't stand |
| | concentrate | unbelievable | settle back |

**What do you think is happening in the pictures? To prepare to listen, make up a story about them with some of the above vocabulary.**

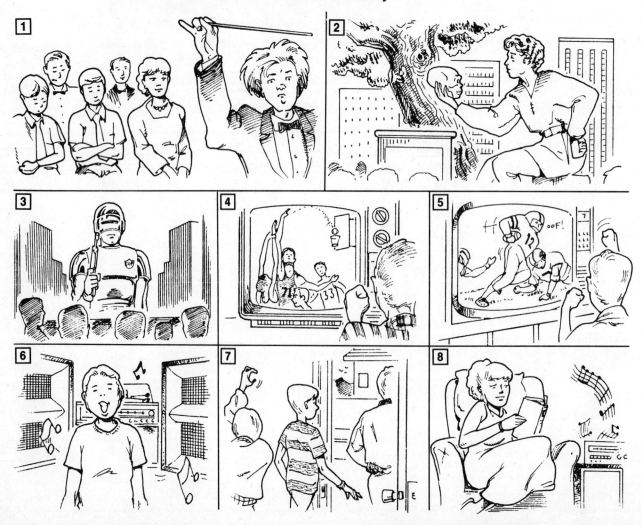

**B.** *Getting the Main Ideas*—Listen to the story, "Sharing Interests." Then circle the letter of the one correct ending for each sentence.

1. The mother is especially concerned about sharing activities with her three children because _____.
   a. she's a single parent
   b. she'd like to participate in sports
   c. they're interested in attending cultural events

2. The mother's and the sons' tastes in movies _____.
   a. are exactly the same
   b. depend on the popular films around town
   c. are quite different

3. When it comes to watching T.V. or listening to music, the three boys _____.
   a. are in complete agreement
   b. tend to argue among themselves
   c. have their mother explain what is going on to them

4. The mother and the sons end up _____.
   a. all going to the movies together
   b. turning off the radio and the T.V. and talking instead
   c. pursuing their individual interests

**C.** Write *M* before the mother's interests and *S* before those of the sons. You may want to listen to the story again.

1. _____ classical music
2. _____ ballet and opera
3. _____ foreign or classic films
4. _____ adventure or horror movies
5. _____ rock music
6. _____ the theater (plays)
7. _____ football
8. _____ basketball

---

### Recognizing Specialized Vocabulary

In talking about special interests or fields of study, speakers may use specialized vocabulary that is not really important to the main ideas of the story. When you hear expressions of this kind, recognizing the general purpose is enough. You don't need to know their specialized meanings to understand the story.

---

**D.** Listen to the story again. Then match these specialized expressions with the areas of interest by writing the letters *a–d* on the lines.

a. "culture"    b. basketball    c. football    d. rock music

1. _b_ half-court offense
2. _____ a thirty-yard outpattern
3. _____ Shakespearean drama
4. _____ fast breaks
5. _____ the echo
6. _____ a field goal
7. _____ the distortion
8. _____ new releases
9. _____ a frozen rope
10. _____ an equalizer

_____ **\*E.** In a few sentences, summarize the story in your own words. (You can look back at the pictures, if necessary.) Try to explain the point. Then you may want to read the note of explanation in the appendix.

_____ **F.** *Telling Your Story*—In the top box under each category, write one of your specific areas of interest (Examples: "culture": ballet; sports: skiing; movies: comedies; music: jazz). Within a time limit, talk to your classmates and find as many as you can who share those specific interests; tally ( ~~||||~~ /// ) the number in the second box.

EXAMPLE:    Student 1: I'm interested in opera. Are you?
Student 2: Not really. I'd rather see a play.
Student 1: Oh. You should talk to Rosa. She likes theater.

**Then answer the questions that follow.**

|  | "culture" | sports | movies | music |
|---|---|---|---|---|
| specific interest |  |  |  |  |
| number who share it |  |  |  |  |

1. How many students shared your interests? Was this most of the students you talked to? If not, about how many was it (about half, a third, a tenth, etc.)? Are your specific interests unusual? If so, why?
2. Do your family members share your interests? Your close friends? Why or why not?
3. In your opinion, is it necessary to share interests to be able to get along well? Why or why not?.

# PART TWO / PRONUNCIATION THROUGH ROLE-PLAY

● Expressing, Accepting, and Turning Down Invitations   ● Recognizing Stress and Pitch Patterns in Phrases

 **A.** **Listen to this conversation.**

**Wife:** I'm bored, and the new neighbors down the street invited us to come by some time. Why don't I call them up now?

**Husband:** Well, I feel like going out, but I don't think we'd get along very well with that couple.

**Wife:** Then I was wondering if you'd like to see that new horror film in town—*Skullbusters*?

**Husband:** I wouldn't mind seeing a movie, but not that one. There wouldn't be any good adventure films or love stories around, would there?

**Wife:** I don't think so. Come on . . . let's put warm jackets on and walk down to the big park on Silver Lake. We could look around for a soccer game to join.

**Husband:** I'd like to, but I'm too tired to run around.

**Wife:** Then would you be interested in sitting down in front of the T.V. set and watching the baseball game together?

**Husband:** I'd be happy to watch a T.V. show, but I can't figure out why you like that sport.

**Wife:** How about turning on the radio and listening to a music station?

**Husband:** I can't stand hearing that country music you like.

**Wife:** Look . . . what would you suggest doing?

**Husband:** Oh, that's up to you. Anything you choose is fine with me.

**Summarize what happened in your own words. Try to explain the point of the story. (Then you may want to read the note of explanation in the appendix.)**

Most verbs and adjectives before prepositions are emphasized. But in most phrasal verbs (*take over, come up, be back, look forward to*, etc.), the primary stress is on the second word, especially if it follows an object or if there is no object. In a phrase with falling intonation, the highest pitch falls on the syllable with the strongest stress.

**B.** Listen to these examples of phrasal verbs. An accent mark ( ´ ) indicates the primary stress in the phrase and a line (____⌐⌐____) shows the pitch (intonation) pattern.

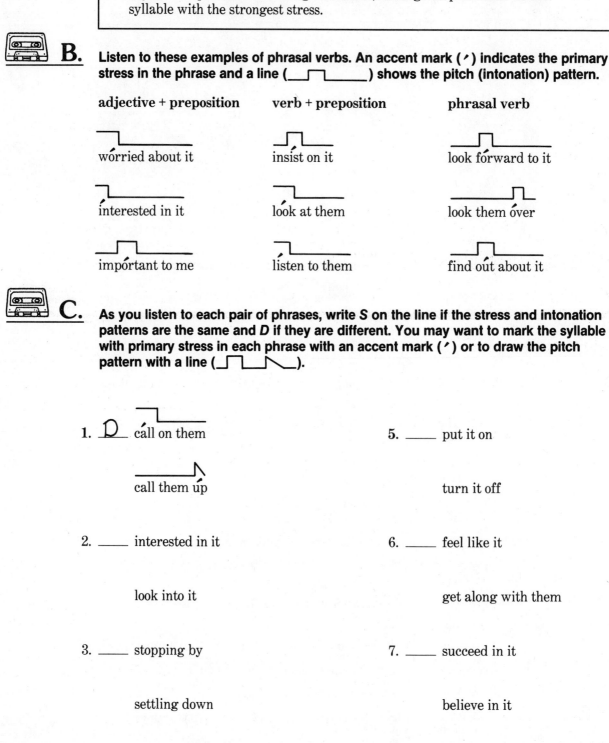

| adjective + preposition | verb + preposition | phrasal verb |
|---|---|---|
| wórried about it | insíst on it | look fórward to it |
| ínterested in it | look át them | look them óver |
| impórtant to me | lísten to them | find óut about it |

**C.** As you listen to each pair of phrases, write *S* on the line if the stress and intonation patterns are the same and *D* if they are different. You may want to mark the syllable with primary stress in each phrase with an accent mark ( ´ ) or to draw the pitch pattern with a line (_⌐⌐_⌐_↘_).

1. _D_ cáll on them

  call them úp

2. ____ interested in it

  look into it

3. ____ stopping by

  settling down

4. ____ listen to them

  argue with them

5. ____ put it on

  turn it off

6. ____ feel like it

  get along with them

7. ____ succeed in it

  believe in it

8. ____ figure it out

  ask about it

> In a noun phrase with an adjective, the primary stress more commonly falls on the noun, but it may fall on either of the words, depending on the speaker's meaning. In a compound noun (two separated or connected words that express one idea), the primary stress usually falls on the first noun.

 **D.** Listen to these examples of adjectives + nouns and of compound nouns.

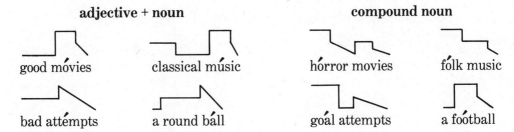

 **E.** As you listen to each pair of phrases, write *S* on the line if the stress and intonation patterns are the same and *D* if they are different. You may want to mark the syllable with primary stress in each phrase with an accent mark or to draw the pitch pattern with a line.

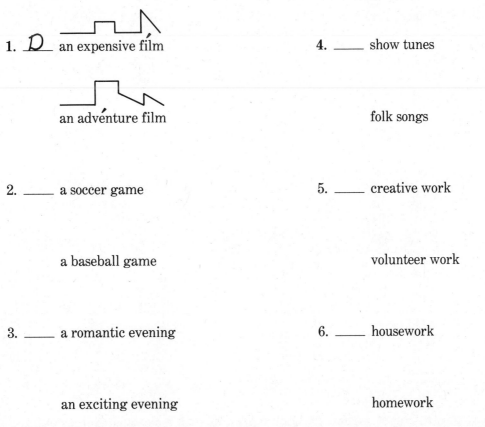

1. *D* ___ an expensive film

   an adventure film

2. ___ a soccer game

   a baseball game

3. ___ a romantic evening

   an exciting evening

4. ___ show tunes

   folk songs

5. ___ creative work

   volunteer work

6. ___ housework

   homework

 **F.** Listen again to the conversation at the beginning of this section (page 89). In each noun, verb, and adjective phrase, you may want to mark the primary stress or to draw a line for the pitch pattern. Then, in pairs, read the conversation aloud.

## G.

*Playing Roles*—**Pay special attention to the primary stress and pitch patterns of phrases as you complete these activities.**

1. In pairs, have the following conversation. The first student begins with the first sentence on the left. The second student chooses and responds with the most appropriate sentences on the right, the first student continues, and so on. You might want to cover the side of the page that your partner is using.

| Student A | Student B |
|---|---|
| Hello, (name), how are you getting along? | A birthday party? When? |
| Friday night around 8:30. | This Friday? Oh, I'm sorry, but my wife (husband) works late at the coffee shop then. She (He) can't make it. |
| Not at all. I've invited classmates, coworkers, and old friends. How about it? | I guess I can then. It sounds like fun. What kind of birthday present would you suggest? |
| That's all right. You can come by without her (him). | Fine, thanks, What's going on with you, (name)? |
| Well, I'm giving a birthday party for my girlfriend (boyfriend), and I was wondering if you'd like to stop by. | Come by myself? Won't everyone be in couples? |

2. Tell some phrases you could use to express, accept, or turn down invitations to share activities. Your instructor will list them on the board. **Examples:**

If you're free then, I'd like to invite you to + NOUN / VERB....
I was wondering if you might like to + VERB....
Would you (by any chance) be interested in + VERBing...?

| | |
|---|---|
| I'd like to, but I can't. | Thank you. I'd love to. |
| I wish I could, but.... | That sounds terrific. |
| Sorry, but I have to + VERB.... | I sure would. What time? |

3. Use the phrases for expressing invitations to get four different classmates to accept your invitation to each of the kinds of activities in this chart. Walk around the classroom to have conversations in pairs. When a classmate accepts, he or she writes his or her name and the details you decided on in the appropriate boxes (**Example:** a sports event: Joe, a soccer game, Saturday morning, 10:00 a.m.). Each student may accept up to four invitations, but only one to each kind of activity.

| | name | kind | day | time |
|---|---|---|---|---|
| a sports event | | | | |
| a concert | | | | |
| a party | | | | |
| a movie | | | | |

## *H.

**Attend one of the activities you agreed on with a classmate, enjoy yourself, and tell the class about it.**

# PART THREE / PRACTICAL LISTENING

● Understanding Descriptions of Sports Events

### Making Inferences

 **A.** Listen to Reports 1–3 twice. The first time, match the reports with the pictures by writing the numbers 1–3 in the boxes. The second time, circle the letter of the sentence that describes the action.

### Report 1

a. The St. Louis team (the Blues) won the game in the last few seconds because their opponents didn't manage to catch a pass.

b. The Minnesota team (the Greens) tied the game because they went for a field goal instead of a touchdown.

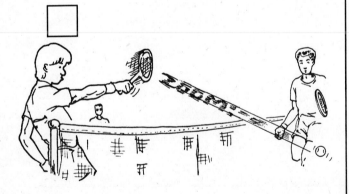

### Report 2

a. Taylor hit a ground ball double off Rick Romero, the pitcher.

b. Romero scored on a fly ball home run after the previous batter struck out.

### Report 3

a. It was near the end of the game, and Decker and McGraw were tied three times.

b. The players were just beginning a new game and set.

**B.** Listen to the description of a baseball field and label the places on the lines after the boxes (□) and the players on the the lines after the circles (○). You can listen again to check your answers.

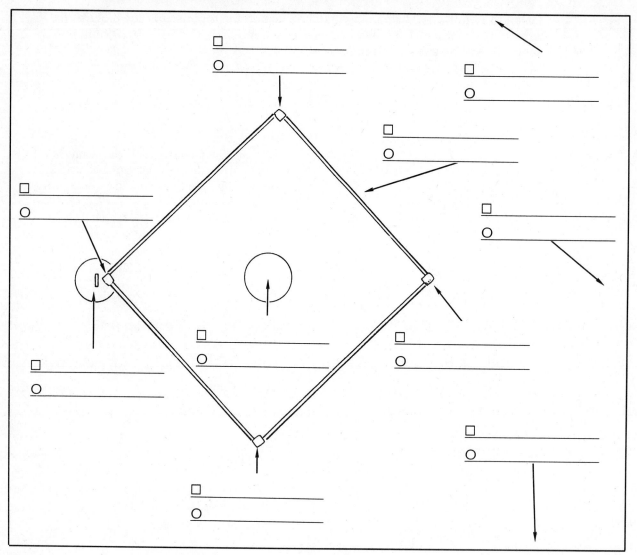

**C.** Listen to the description of the rules of baseball and answer these questions. (Write only the important words to summarize the rules.) You can listen again to check your answers. Discuss the rules with the class.

1. How does a team score runs? _____

_____

2. How can the defensive team prevent the team at bat from scoring? _____

_____

3. How does the pitcher strike out a batter? _____

_____

4. Who wins the game? _____

_____

> To understand the events in a narration, you may not need to know the exact meanings of the specific vocabulary. But if you want to learn more about the activity or area of interest, you might write down the words and expressions you don't understand and find out what they mean.

 **D.** **Listen again to the sports reports and descriptions in this section. Then list some of the specialized vocabulary on the lines. Explain the items that you understand and ask your classmates the meanings of the others.**

**EXAMPLE:** I understand that a *field goal* means "kicking the football through the goal posts," but what does *third down and eight* mean?

football                            tennis                          baseball

1. _field goal_ _____    _____    _____

2. _third down and eight_ _____    _____    _____

3. _____    _____    _____

4. _____    _____    _____

**\*E.** **Beyond the text: Videotape or tape record part of a sports event from T.V. or radio. Play it in class and summarize what happened. Write down some of the specialized vocabulary and explain or ask about it.**

# PART FOUR / LANGUAGE ACTIVITIES

● Understanding and Describing the Rules of Games

**A.** In pairs, explain one of these sports diagrams to your partner. Your partner will explain the other diagram to you.

EXAMPLE:   In a basketball court, there is a basket at each end line. The free throw line is fifteen feet from the basket.

1.

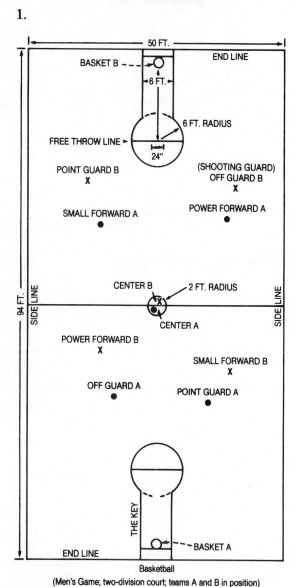

Basketball
(Men's Game; two-division court; teams A and B in position)

2.

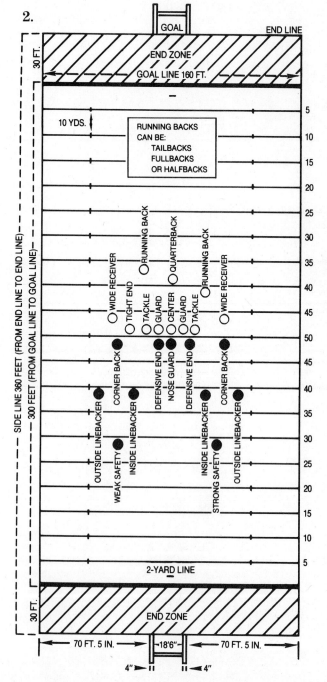

**\*B.** Draw the field or court for a sport that you know and label the important places and players. Don't show your partner your diagram but describe it. Your partner will draw a diagram from your description and then compare it with yours. He or she will try to explain the diagram to the class.

> To explain how to do something in a sport, game, or other recreational activity, you should describe the steps as precisely as possible in chronological order.

## C. Follow these steps to give a short speech about an activity.

1. Choose a "how to" topic that is part of a sport or game. Be sure that the activity is specific enough to describe in less than five minutes. **Examples:**

   - how to hit a baseball
   - how to catch a fly ball
   - how to dribble a basketball
   - how to shoot a basket
   - how to lift a barbell
   - how to roller-skate
   - how to ski

   - how to kick a field goal
   - how to swing a tennis racket
   - how to drive a golf ball
   - how to bowl
   - how to ride a bicycle
   - how to play jacks
   - how to shuffle a deck of cards

2. In small groups, pantomime your activity by showing the movements without speaking. Then describe the steps in order. **Example:**

   To play jacks, first you scatter the jacks on the floor or table.

   Make sure they're not too far apart.

   Next, put the ball in one hand and toss it into the air.

   Before it bounces, try to pick up one jack with the same hand.

   You have to catch the ball in the same hand, too.

   Put each jack you pick up in your other hand.

   Repeat these steps until you've picked up all the jacks, one at a time.

   If you miss, another player gets a turn.

   After you pick up all the jacks, one by one in one turn, repeat the game but this time, pick up two jacks each time you toss the ball.

   The next time, pick up the jacks by threes, then by fours, etc.

3. Prepare a short talk on the activity for the class. You can bring objects (a ball, a bat, a tennis racket, etc.) and have a partner pantomime the steps in the actions as you explain them.

4. Give the talk and have the class show they understand by summarizing the steps in order. (Listeners may take notes during the speeches.)

5. Outside or in a place that's safe for sports or recreational activities, play some of the games with your classmates.

# The Media

**COMPETENCIES:** Understanding and expressing opinions
Recognizing support for an opinion
Expressing opinions, agreeing, and disagreeing
Determining supporting reasons for an opinion
Summarizing the plot of a story
Debating issues

**PRONUNCIATION:** Recognizing phrase and sentence rhythm

**GRAMMAR FOCUS:** The passive

# PART ONE / LEARNING TO LISTEN

● Understanding and Expressing Opinions  ● Recognizing Support for an Opinion

## Vocabulary and Prelistening

**A.**  **Read the words and phrases. (You may want to pronounce them and discuss the meanings.)**

| Nouns | Verbs | Adjectives/Adverbs | Expressions/Idioms |
|---|---|---|---|
| roommate | fade | unhealthy | turn to |
| muscles | ruin | passively | murder mystery |
| complexion | destroy | intriguing | T.V. viewing |
| eyesight | communicate | absolutely | educational system |
| reply | question | fascinating | witness stand |
| brain | hypnotize | sarcastic | commit a murder |
| creativity | interrupt | declining | commercial T.V. |
| failure | present | entire | in poor taste |
| intelligence | yawn | impatiently | solve a case |
| similarities | accuse | insulting | attempt on a life |
| plot | discover | boring | cut off from |
| argument | ignore | astounding | "on a roll" |
| reality | manipulate | enthusiastic | turns out |
| dial | persuade | confident | get a point across |

**What do you think is happening in the pictures? To prepare to listen, make up a story about them with some of the above vocabulary.**

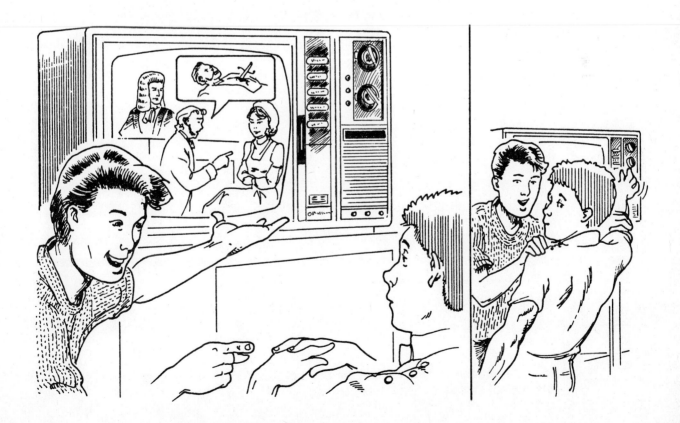

**B.**   *Getting the Main Ideas*—Listen to the story, "Opinions about Television." Then circle the letter of the one correct phrase that completes each sentence.

1. The speaker expresses the opinion that watching T.V. is _____.
   a. fascinating, creative, and educational
   b. unhealthy, boring, and insulting to the intelligence
   c. good for you if you choose programs carefully

2. When the speaker tells his views, his roommate Walter _____.
   a. absolutely agrees with his opinions
   b. strongly disagrees with him
   c. may or may not agree, but isn't very strong in his opinions

3. Walter is more interested in _____ than in arguing about the advantages and disadvantages of T.V. viewing.
   a. telling his roommate the plot of the mystery he's watching
   b. turning off the set to get some exercise
   c. listening to a football game on the radio

---

### Recognizing Support for an Opinion

When expressing personal judgments, speakers usually give reasons for their points of view. This support can consist of facts or opinions.

---

**C.**   Listen to the story again. Then complete the speaker's opinions by writing the important words on the lines.

1. While you're sitting passively in front of the T.V. set, your muscles _____

   _____, your complexion _____,

   and your eyesight _____.

2. It seems to me that the brain _____.

3. In my opinion, creativity _____, and people

   _____.

4. From my point of view, T.V. is the cause of _____

   _____.

5. The way I feel about it, the programs presented on commercial T.V. _____

   _____. I find them _____.

6. As I see it, not only _____ but viewers are

   also _____.

7. As far as I'm concerned, I'd say that T.V. watchers _____

   _____.

_____ **\*D.**   In a few sentences try to explain the point of the story. (Then you may want to read the note of explanation in the appendix.)

**E.**   *Telling Your Story*—The two characters in the story "Opinions about Television" keep trying to talk about different topics. To play a conversation game, follow these steps.

1. Choose a topic related to the media (**Examples:** T.V. sports, a T.V. program you liked, music on your favorite radio station, the news on National Public Radio, a magazine article you've read). Make some notes for yourself about the topic (What might you say about it?).

2. In pairs, follow these rules to talk about your topic: Don't interrupt your partner when he or she is talking. Keep your "speeches" short. Don't talk more than a half minute before giving your partner a chance. When you begin to talk, relate your topic to what your partner has just said in some way. **Examples:**

**Student 1** (*topic = a magazine article about snakes*):
I read a fascinating article in *National Geographic*. It's about snakes.

**Student 2** (*topic = a T.V. detective drama*):
Uh-huh. There are people who can be considered snakes, too. For instance, in the T.V. detective story I saw last night, there was a businessman who did terrible things.

**Student 1:**   I see. Well, the article said that some people have discovered that snakes can be used in business.

3. Answer these questions for the class: Who was more successful in talking about his or her topic? Why?

# PART TWO / PRONUNCIATION THROUGH ROLE-PLAY

● Expressing Opinions, Agreeing, and Disagreeing   ● Recognizing Phrase and Sentence Rhythm

 **A.**   **Listen to this conversation.**

**Roommate 1:**  It seems to me that if your programs are chosen carefully, T.V. viewing can be considered very educational.

**Roommate 2:**  I couldn't agree with you more.

**Roommate 1:**  If you ask me, excellent cultural shows are presented on the public broadcasting network.

**Roommate 2:**  You're absolutely right.

**Roommate 1:**  From my point of view, you have to watch T.V. to be well informed these days, right?

**Roommate 2:**  I agree with you completely.

**Roommate 1:**  The way I feel about it, our system of government depends on informing the public. In my opinion, democracy couldn't exist without the mass media. I find T.V. essential!

**Roommate 2:**  I feel exactly the same way!

**Roommate 1:**  So let's spend the evening watching a ballet performance—followed by a political debate.

**Roommate 2:**  What? No way! I want to see the basketball game!

**Summarize what happened in your own words. Try to explain the point of the story. (Then you may want to read the note of explanation in the appendix.)**

> The rhythm of phrases and sentences in spoken English depends on the number of stressed syllables. Two groups of words with the same number of emphasized syllables are pronounced in about the same amount of time. If there are unstressed syllables, they are spoken quickly. If a phrase or sentence contains only stressed syllables, they are stretched out to fill time.

 **B.** **Listen to these examples of phrase and sentence rhythm. A line ( ‿‿‿ ) indicates the amount of time between stressed syllables. Notice that in each group the phrases or sentences have the same number of stressed syllables (time intervals) but different numbers of unstressed ones.**

Watching     television is unhealthy.

Your   muscles   are   turning   to   fat.

Creativity     is     killed   by   T.V.

watch          good          shows

watching   a   good          show

watch   a   good          program

watching   an   excellent   program

I'm   watching   an   excellent   program.

 **C.** **As you listen to each pair of phrases or sentences, write _S_ on the line if the phrases or sentences are pronounced in about the same amount of time (if there are the same number of stressed syllables). Write _D_ on the line if the rhythms of the phrases or sentences are different.**

1. __S__ excellent cultural shows / interesting media news

2. _____ if you ask me / as far as I'm concerned

3. _____ the way I feel / my point of view

4. _____ the public network / a private channel

5. _____ Radio can be educational. / T.V. insults the intelligence.

6. _____ Turn off the set, please. / Could you change the channel?

7. _____ You're absolutely correct. / I absolutely agree.

8. _____ I think you're wrong. / I feel you're right.

 **D.** **Listen again to the conversation at the beginning of this section (page 102). You may want to draw a line ( ‿‿‿ ) for the rhythm pattern. Then, in pairs, read the conversation aloud.**

## E.  *Playing Roles*—Pay special attention to phrase and sentence rhythm as you complete these activities.

1. In groups of three, have the following conversation in several different ways. Each time, choose different phrases.

**Student 1:**

| In my opinion,<br>As I see it,<br>From my point of view,<br>The way I feel, | our level of education | is being decreased<br>has been lowered | by | T.V. viewing.<br>television.<br>insulting shows. |

**Student 2:** I absolutely agree.
I couldn't agree with you more.
I feel exactly the same way.
I kind of see your point.

**Student 3:**

| I don't know.<br>I'm not sure.<br>Wait a minute.<br>Hold on. | You may have a point,<br>You could be right in a way,<br>I understand your point of view,<br>I see what you mean, | but | it seems to me<br>if you ask me,<br>as far as I'm concerned,<br>I think |

| television has contributed | to | our democratic system of government.<br>our rich cultural life.<br>our comfortable way of life.<br>communication among different groups of people. |

2. Tell some phrases you could use to express opinions and to agree and politely disagree with them. Your instructor will list them on the board. **Examples:**

| I'm of the opinion that... | Personally,... |
| From my point of view,... | Speaking for myself,... |

| I agree with you completely. | I see your point, but I think... |
| That's a good point. | I can't entirely agree with you. |
| That's for sure. | Sorry, but I'm not sure I agree. |

3. Work in pairs. For each of the following statements, add a phrase to show that it is your personal opinion. (You may have to make the statement negative or change it in some other way to be truthful.) Your partner will agree or disagree with the opinion you express and tell why. **Example:**

**Student 1:** If you ask me, too much T.V. viewing is bad for the health.

**Student 2:** I see your point—if you sit sit for hours without moving when you watch television. But I can't entirely agree with you. It seems to me that you can get valuable information about health from T.V. and you can do exercises when watching exercise shows.

   a. Too much T.V. viewing is bad for the health.
   b. Murder mysteries are intriguing because they aren't insulting to the intelligence.
   c. Many of the programs presented on commercial T.V. are in poor taste or are badly written and produced.
   d. Viewers are manipulated psychologically when they watch T.V.
   e. T.V. watchers are cut off from reality.
   f. Excellent cultural shows are presented on the public broadcasting network.
   g. You have to watch T.V. to be well informed these days.
   h. Democracy couldn't exist without the mass media.

# PART THREE / PRACTICAL LISTENING

● Determining Supporting Reasons for an Opinion ● Summarizing the Plot of a Story

> ### Making Inferences
>
> Most speakers who express their opinions indicate the supporting reason(s) for these viewpoints.

 **A.** **Read these sentences. Then listen to Opinions 1–3 twice. The first time, cross out the incorrect word(s) in the summary sentence. The second time, circle the letter of the speaker's supporting reason.**

## Opinion 1

*Summary Sentence:*
The speaker [likes/~~doesn't like~~] T.V. soap operas.

*Reason:*
a. They are an escape from the problems of the real world.
b. They deal fairly realistically with important social issues.
c. The strongest characters are the ones with negative social characteristics—dishonesty, lack of caring about others, etc.

## Opinion 2

*Summary Sentence:*
The speaker [approves/doesn't approve] of T.V. for young children.

a. It has many advantages in elementary school education.
b. It destroys their ability to imagine and to concentrate.
c. It improves reading skills because kindergartners are taught to pay attention and to listen carefully.

## Opinion 3

*Summary Sentence:*
The speaker [thinks/doesn't think] that the mass media influences politics positively.

*Reason:*
a. Social change is brought about by groups of people, not by television or radio.
b. Viewers are encouraged to read more about the events they've seen on T.V.
c. T.V. watchers are involved in current events soon after the news is made.

> Many people enjoy talking about T.V. shows they have seen. They summarize the plot of the story (the important events), usually in the present tenses, and tell why they liked the program.

 **B.** **Listen to the plot summary of "The Printer's Devil" twice. The first time, cross out the three events below that did not happen in the story. The second time, number the other six events in order.**

\_\_\_\_\_ Events (all terrible disasters) are being reported on before they even happen.

\_\_\_\_\_ A man named Smith stops him before he commits suicide.

\_\_\_\_\_ ~~Smith buys the newspaper from the editor for the syndicate.~~

\_\_\_\_\_ The editor of a small newspaper is being driven out of business by a big syndicate.

_1_ The newspaper fails because Smith can't operate the machines very quickly and doesn't get big stories.

\_\_\_\_\_ The small newspaper becomes successful again because Smith is able to turn out papers with astounding headlines at an amazing speed.

\_\_\_\_\_ Smith gets the paper out of debt and begins working for the editor for free.

\_\_\_\_\_ The editor signs a contract with Smith (who is really the devil).

\_\_\_\_\_ The contract has no meaning because Smith is not a human being, and the story has a happy ending.

\_\_\_\_\_ **C.** **In small groups, take turns summarizing the plot of a T.V. program with a story that you enjoyed. If the group members don't understand what happened, they should ask about the details. Of the programs described, choose one that everyone in the group found interesting and have one student summarize it for the class. Then ask the class these questions: According to the description, what might you think of the program (Examples: that it is fascinating, that it is insulting to the intelligence, that it is boring)? Why?**

\_\_\_\_\_ **\*D.** **Beyond the text: In class, watch a T.V. program that has a story or videotape one and play the tape in class. During the commercials and after the show, summarize the plot. Then discuss your opinions of the show.**

# PART FOUR / LANGUAGE ACTIVITIES

● Debating Issues

> In a formal debate, two groups of speakers argue opposing sides of an issue in turn.

## A.  To have a class debate on a media issue, follow these steps.

1. Check the statements about television that you agree with and write *0* before those statements that you disagree with.

   _____ Too much T.V. viewing is bad for the health.

   _____ T.V. watchers are cut off from reality.

   _____ Excellent cultural shows are presented on the public broadcasting network.

   _____ You have to watch T.V. to be well informed these days.

   _____ Democracy couldn't exist without the mass media.

   _____ Our democratic system is being destroyed because viewers are manipulated (told what to think) by the broadcast media (T.V. and radio).

   _____ The mass media leaves no room for cultural diversity.

   _____ Television is the main cause of the failure of our school systems to educate students.

   _____ The broadcast media should be used by the schools as the basis of our educational system.

   _____ One of the best ways to learn a new language is to watch T.V. and to listen to the radio.

   _____ T.V. programs must be written and produced for the general public—to appeal to the tastes of the masses.

   _____ T.V. and radio should be publicly funded, and networks should not be allowed to sell commercial advertising.

   _____ Commercials are a good example of a creative, effective use of the media.

   _____ Networks should not be permitted to present shows that include violence.

   _____ There should be no censorship (control of material) in the media; the public must be allowed to choose what it wants to see and hear.

2. From your answers in Step 1, decide whether you agree or disagree with this statement: The broadcast media of the United States and Canada are generally beneficial to society.

3. Divide the class into two groups: students who agree with the statement in Step 2 and students who disagree with it. If the groups are not approximately the same size, some students will have to join the other group to make them equal.

4. In your separate groups, discuss and list reasons that support your point of view (for or against the statement in Step 2.) Arrange them in logical order. Then divide them into five groups of related points. **Examples:**

### Group 1: FOR

1. T.V. and radio present news as it happens. Viewers are a part of current events. The media influences history and is the basis of democracy.

2. The mass media brings the world closer together. It helps people in different cultures to understand one another.

### Group 2: AGAINST

1. T.V. and radio should simply report the news objectively. They should not influence public opinion. The public is being manipulated.

2. The mass media creates cultural uniformity. It destroys differences in social class, culture, and values.

Choose five students as speakers to present the five groups of supporting points in the formal debate.

5. In the middle of the room, arrange ten chairs in two rows of five seats each, facing each other, for the five speakers of each group.

6. The first of the five speakers in the "for" row briefly summarizes his or her points. The class takes notes. One or two students from the "for" group in the class adds explanation to those points, and one or two students from the "against" group responds.

7. The first of the five speakers in the "against" row briefly summarizes his or her points. The class takes notes. One or two students from the "against" group in the class adds explanation to those points, and one or two students from the "for" group responds.

8. Steps 6 and 7 are repeated for each of the remaining four speakers on each side.

9. The class briefly summarizes the main arguments of the "for" side and the main arguments for the "against" side. The instructor lists these main points on the board.

10. The class votes on the "winner" of the debate (the side with the stronger arguments) and discusses the reasons for the vote.

## *B. To have another class debate, follow these steps:

1. As a class, decide on a statement of opinion about a current issue. (You may get ideas from the material in other chapters of this book.) **Examples:**

It is difficult for immigrants and foreign students to get to know North Americans because North Americans are unfriendly to people of other cultures.

Education is a privilege, not a right; taxpayers should not have to pay for public education.

The United States (or Canada) is too capitalistic; the entire culture is based on money.

Workers have too many rights in this society, and their power harms the economic system.

The legal system in this country is an unfair one: only the rich can afford justice.

Travel is the best way to educate yourself about other cultures and to contribute to understanding in the world.

Men and women are so different that they can never be equal.

Competitive sports are too important in this country.

2. Divide the class into two groups: students who agree with the statement and students who disagree. If the groups are not approximately the same size, some students will have to join the other group to make them equal.

3. Follow Steps 4–10 in Activity A.

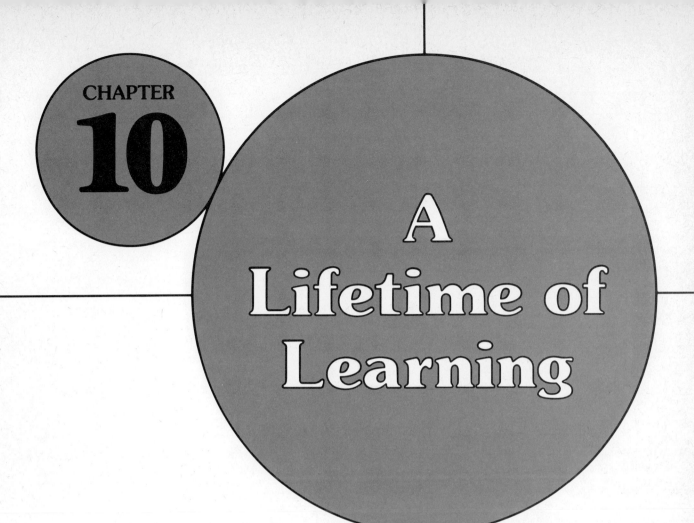

CHAPTER

# 10

# A Lifetime of Learning

**COMPETENCIES:** Recognizing the structure of a short speech
Giving a short speech
Recognizing ways to improve language skills
Understanding some views on language
Understanding rules of some common word games
Playing a question-and-answer game

**PRONUNCIATION:** Recognizing sentence focus

**GRAMMAR FOCUS:** Noun, adjective, and adverb clauses

# PART ONE / LEARNING TO LISTEN

● Recognizing the Structure of a Short Speech   ● Giving a Short Speech

## Vocabulary and Prelistening

_____ **A.** **Read the words and phrases. (You may want to pronounce them and discuss the meanings.)**

| Nouns | | Verbs | Adjectives/Adverbs |
|---|---|---|---|
| clerk | confidence | pronounce | embarrassed |
| counter | accent | improve | particularly |
| shelf | grammar | notice | |
| pepper | mistakes | wonder | **Expressions/Idioms** |
| repeats | impression | practice | corner grocery store |
| | | | quiet and shy |

**What do you think is happening in the pictures? To prepare to listen, make up a story about them with some of the above vocabulary.**

**B.**  *Getting the Main Ideas*—Listen to the story, "Improving Language Skills." Then circle the letter of the one correct ending for each sentence.

1. Before she came to the United States, the speaker _____.
   a. had never spoken English to an American before
   b. had studied English with a Canadian college professor
   c. had learned practical English vocabulary for everyday life

2. On her second day here, she brought home the wrong item from the corner grocery store because she _____.
   a. hadn't eaten American food before
   b. was embarrassed about her pronunciation
   c. hadn't understood her mother's shopping list

3. She improved her English by _____.
   a. participating in sports events—soccer, tennis, and baseball
   b. watching, listening to, and reading the same information in different forms of the media
   c. teaching her language at the local adult school

4. She used to give the impression of being quiet and shy because _____.
   a. she spoke so carefully that she rarely made a mistake
   b. she knew that American men liked women who didn't talk much
   c. she spoke softly so no one would notice her mistakes

5. Besides improving her language skills at work, she'll be getting practice in English every day after she _____.
   a. goes back to her country
   b. leaves her office job
   c. gets married to her American boyfriend

---

### Recognizing the Structure of a Short Speech

A formal speech on any topic should be organized so that listeners can follow the main ideas. It may be divided into parts—each about a different part of the topic.

---

**C.**  Listen to the speech again. Complete these notes about the five parts of the story by writing the important words on the lines.

1. a story about when the speaker _____

   _____

2. ways that the speaker _____

3. why her American boyfriend _____

   _____

4. how she practices _____

5. what will happen after _____

_____ **\*D.**   **Use your notes in Exercise C to summarize the story in the order the speaker told it. (In one or two sentences, tell the important details in each of the five parts of the story.) Then try to explain the point. (Then you may want to read the note of explanation in the appendix.)**

_____ **\*E.**   *Telling Your Story*—**To give a short speech to the class, follow these steps.**

1. Choose a topic related to language learning (**Examples:** how I've been learning English, why English is difficult for me, the differences between English and my language, how I would teach a language class).

2. Divide your topic into three to six parts and write a phrase for each part on a separate note card. On each card, list notes about the details of that part. (Don't write the sentences of your speech, just notes about the important details.)

3. In turn, give a speech on your topic, of about two to five minutes, to the class. You can use your notes for help, but be sure to speak directly to your listeners. The class can take notes.

4. The class will summarize the main points of your speech and ask you questions. Answer them with more information.

# PART TWO / PRONUNCIATION THROUGH ROLE-PLAY

● Recognizing Ways to Improve Language Skills  ● Recognizing Sentence Focus

 **A.**    **Listen to this conversation.**

Student:  Can you tell us how we can improve our language skills?

Instructor:  I'd like to be able to say that there are specific methods that work with all language learners, but there aren't.

Student:  You mean there's nothing we can do to learn English better?

Instructor:  There's plenty you can do. First, you can listen.

Student:  Listen to what?

Instructor:  Listen to your instructor, your coworkers, neighbors, friends, and the broadcast media. And after you listen, you can talk.

Student:  Talk about what?

Instructor:  About school, work, current events and issues, opinions, and ideas.

Student:  But how can we learn the vocabulary we need to talk?

Instructor:  By listening and reading. And reading will help you if you want to write, too. You learn a language best when you use it in your everyday life.

Student:  But how can I use English if everyone in my neighborhood speaks my native language?

Instructor:  If you got involved, you'd learn English faster.

Student:  Involved in what?

Instructor:  In the culture of English. Right now, let's divide the class into groups.

Student:  What are the groups supposed to do?

Instructor:  You're supposed to brainstorm ideas on how to improve your language skills.

**Summarize the conversation in your own words. Try to explain the point. (Then you may want to read the note of explanation in the appendix.)**

> In normal sentence rhythm, the last content word (noun, verb, adjective, or adverb) usually has the strongest emphasis. But to emphasize another word that is more important, a speaker will stress it even more. For example, the words that introduce a new idea, perhaps in contrast to previous information, will often have the strongest stress.

 **B.**    **Listen to these examples of important, stressed words. The focus (the word with the strongest stress in a phrase or sentence) is in CAPITAL LETTERS.**

Student:  Can you explain how I can improve my WRITING?

Instructor:  You'll learn to write better if you PRACTICE.

Student:  Practice WHAT?

Instructor:  Your WRITING. Try writing in a JOURNAL every day.

Student:  What's a JOURNAL?

Instructor:  It's a book of YOUR writing.

Student: What KIND of writing?

Instructor: PERSONAL writing--your thoughts for THAT day.

Student: Thoughts about WHAT?

Instructor: About ANYTHING—a memory, your reaction to an event, a new idea—
whatever comes to MIND.

 **C.** **As you listen to this conversation, underline the word that is the focus of each phrase or sentence.**

Student: Will you correct it?

Instructor: Correct what?

Student: The journal that I write.

Instructor: I will if you want me to, but I'd rather just read it, not correct it.

Student: Why won't you correct my mistakes?

Instructor: Because you'll improve your English if you just express yourself without
worrying about every word or sentence.

Student: Express myself about what?

Instructor: About anything that interests you that day.

Student: Can you suggest some topics?

Instructor: I can, but you should write down your own thoughts.

 **D.** **Listen again to the conversation at the beginning of this section (page 113). You may want to underline the word that is the focus of each phrase or sentence. Then, in pairs, read the conversation aloud.**

**E.** *Playing Roles*—**Pay special attention to phrase and sentence focus as you complete these activities.**

1. In groups, follow these steps to brainstorm ideas in answer to this question: How can you improve your language skills?

   • Express as many ideas as you think of within a time limit (about ten minutes). Don't worry about correctness or whether or not the ideas are good ones.
   • Don't respond to anyone else's ideas.
   • One student should write the ideas down.

2. Discuss the ideas in your list, and have one student check ( ✓ ) the ten that the group agrees are the best. **Examples:**

   Join a singing or dancing group.          Look up every word you hear in a dictionary.
   Teach an American your language.        To yourself, repeat everything your instructor says.
   Fall in love with an American.              Work part-time job where everyone speaks English.
   Take an acting class.                            Play word games.
   Learn the words of songs and sing them when you drive.
   Read at least one news article every day. Summarize it in writing. Then listen to the
   same news on the radio and on T.V.

3. In turn, each group tells the class one of its ideas, and the instructor lists them on the board, leaving out repeats.

4. Discuss the ideas listed on the board and have your instructor check the best ones. Then try the ideas that you think might work for you.

# PART THREE / PRACTICAL LISTENING

● Understanding Some Views on Language  ● Understanding Rules of Some Common Word Games

 **A.**    *Making Inferences—Read these sentences. Then listen to Stories 1–3. For each story, circle the letters of two inferences you can make from it. You can listen again to check your answers.*

## Story 1

*Possible Inferences:*

a. The speaker's daughter speaks out in class and doesn't work as hard in school as she should.

b. The speaker can't understand anything the teacher says because he hasn't learned English very well himself.

c. The maximum capacity of a superior learner is fulfilled when a student is motivated to stagnate through curriculum innovation.

d. Experts in education may use jargon (specialized language that people outside the field may find difficult to understand).

## Story 2

*Possible Inferences:*

a. A man should break up with his girlfriend if she's too good for him and she wants her freedom.

b. If you don't take the feelings of a friend who is sad seriously, you won't help him or her to feel better.

c. Someone who is feeling miserable probably needs a friend who will listen and make suggestions.

d. True love among fish in the sea never lasts forever.

## Story 3

*Possible Inferences:*

a. Adults learn foreign languages better than children because they study what their instructors have assigned.

b. Students who learn on their own and communicate in English outside of class will improve faster than those who don't.

c. Chinese is more difficult than English because you can't "talk around" what you want to express.

d. Successful language learners try to guess at meanings and figure out rules for themselves, even if they make mistakes.

> You can improve your language skills through games, and there are many oral word games that are easy to learn and play.

 **B.**    **As you listen to the students playing these word games, try to figure out the rules and complete these sentences that explain them. You can listen again to check your answers.**

## Game 1

1. The first player completes the sentence, "I bought . . . at the store" with a word that

   begins with _____.

2. The second player repeats what _____ and adds a

   word that _____.

3. The third player _____ and adds

   _____.

4. Continue the chain until _____

   _____.

5. Review the chain by beginning with ____ and _____

   _____.

### Game 2

1. The first player begins the game with _____ that could start a sentence.
2. The second player says _____ that could follow _____

   _____ logically.
3. The third player says _____.
4. Continue the game until _____.
5. Then repeat the whole _____.

### Game 3

1. The first player makes up a two-clause sentence that begins with the connecting word

   _____.

2. The second player makes the second clause of the first sentence into a clause that _____

   _____ and completes the sentence with another clause.

3. The third player _____

   _____.

4. Continue the game until the story _____.
5. Begin a new story with _____.

**\*C.**    **In class, play the games in Exercise B. Then suggest other oral word games and play one of them each day.**

# PART FOUR / LANGUAGE ACTIVITIES

● Playing a Question-and-Answer Game

> Language has different purposes, one of which is to find out about other
> people from what they say.

**A.** **To play a question-and-answer game that will help you to get to know one another well, divide into groups. The first player in each group chooses one of the following questions and answers it, telling his or her reasons. The other players discuss the answer, telling whether they agree or disagree and why. The next player chooses a different question to answer, the group discusses it, and so on.**

1. If a stranger were being attacked by a dangerous-looking criminal and needed help, what would you do?
2. If you were offered $100,000 to pose nude (with no clothing) in a magazine, would you take the job?
3. If your best friend's mother (or father) made a pass at you (indicated that she or he were interested in you romantically), would you tell your friend about it?
4. If you knew your boss was stealing money from the company account but that you would lose your job by reporting him or her, what would you do?
5. If an acquaintance had body odor that you knew was affecting his or her business success and social life, would you tell him or her what the problem was?
6. If you had proposals of marriage from a very rich person whom you didn't love and a very poor one whom you did, which would you choose?
7. If you had to make the choice of becoming blind, deaf, or crippled, which would you choose?
8. If you had the chance to change something that happened to you in the past, what event would you choose?
9. If you could acquire one talent without attending school or practicing, what ability would it be?
10. If you knew that you had only a short time to live, what would you do?

**\*B.** **Write several questions of your own that require honest answers about values, each on a separate slip of paper. Your instructor will collect the papers, mix them up, and put them in a box or bag. In groups or as a class, each student in turn picks a slip of paper, reads aloud the question, and answers it, following the instructions in Exercise A.**

# Appendix / The Points of the Stories

## CHAPTER 1 / MEETING PEOPLE

### Part One, Exercise D:

A charming trick to meet someone new might be fun, but it isn't necessary and it may not work. Most people prefer a direct, simple approach.

### Part Two, Exercise A:

Some people believe they have to lie or flatter someone to attract attention, but most people would prefer an honest "opening line" and a simple, direct approach.

## CHAPTER 2 / GETTING AN EDUCATION

### Part One, Exercise E:

The educational process may vary in different cultures, and students may need some time to get used to it. But they should ask questions—of their classmates, instructors, and counselors.

### Part Two, Exercise A:

Most instructors in the United States and Canada expect and welcome class participation. If the class is silent after a lecture, they may think that the students are uninterested in the topic. But of course they can't answer more than one question at a time.

## CHAPTER 3 / MONEY, MONEY, MONEY

### Part One, Exercise D:

Even if their income is adequate and they understand banking, some people have money problems. Because of the charge-account and credit system in this country, they get into financial difficulty and don't know how to get out of it.

### Part Two, Exercise A:

The number of questions to answer and choices to make in financial matters in the United States may surprise some newcomers.

### Part Four, Exercise A:

These statements are good advice: 2, 3, 5, 9, 11. Taking the other suggestions could cost you money or damage your credit rating.

## CHAPTER 4 / EARNING A LIVING

### Part Two, Exercise A:

Workers in any business are responsible for taking precautions and for following the safety instructions of their supervisors.

### Part Four, Exercise A:

(suggested solutions to problems)

1. The basis of most business organizations is the use of authority, and employees unwilling to follow the instructions of their supervisors are likely to lose their jobs. Even if you don't have the power to fire workers in your department, you don't have to accept an uncooperative attitude. It's your responsibility to make sure the work gets done, so you should give out assignments politely but directly. For example, you ought to say, "I'd like you to handle this on your own," or "I need this work completed by 5:00 today." You can add, "If there is a problem, let me know," but the idea is to expect employees to follow your orders.

2. Your attitude is understandable, and you shouldn't make any effort to "cover for" an inefficient employee who isn't doing her share of the work. On the other hand, you weren't hired to be her supervisor, so it's not your responsibility to criticize. It's up to the owner of the company to judge the quality of all his or her employees' contributions and to take action if necessary.

3. No employee is required to socialize with his or her coworkers, so you don't have to make an effort to "fit in" if you don't want to. Try not to confuse work place relationships with true, long-lasting friendships. Of course, to keep the atmosphere pleasant and to be able to complete assignments in a cooperative way, you'll probably choose to maintain friendly relationships with your coworkers. It should be easy to make social conversation about the interests that you do have in common—your work and your employer.

## CHAPTER 5 / GETTING HELP

### Part One, Exercise D:

Although there are some situations in which a lawyer's services are essential, many minor matters can be handled by the people involved. The teller of this story, however, intends to get free advice from attorneys when she takes care of legal matters herself.

### Part Two, Exercise A:

The police don't consider ignorance of the law a valid reason for breaking it, and some laws may surprise you. It's a good idea to know your basic responsibilities, rights, and protections in case you are stopped by an officer or arrested (taken into custody).

### Part Two, Exercise B:

There are many legal situations in which an attorney is not needed to represent you in court, but you may need information from an attorney to be able to decide which situations these are.

### Part Three, Exercise B:

In a similiar case that came to court, the judge ruled in favor of the plaintiff, but only for the amount of $75—the difference between the highest current selling price of an automobile of that make, model, and year and the insurance company's offer. The law in most states limits the amount to be paid for car damage to its current market value. The defendant did not have to pay for the car to be rebuilt because the plaintiff had not given any special reasons or brought along any expert witnesses to prove that it was worth more than the usual amount.

### Part Four, Exercise A:

Here are results in similiar cases that went to court.

### Case 1:

The judge ruled in favor of the plaintiff, who should have the right to choose a convenient repair shop that he knew and trusted. The court felt that the word "replacement" in the insurance policy could mean "new or used parts" and that a new car should have new ones. The plaintiff was awarded $785, the the average repair estimate minus the $50 deductible.

### Case 2:

There was no need for a verdict in this case because the plaintiff and the defendant worked out their differences during the hearing. The defendant agreed to get a new insurance claim form from the firm, fill out the personal information and sign it, and give it to the dentist's receptionist to send in. The dentist agreed to adjust the dentures so they would fit, and the defendant made an appointment for the next day.

### Case 3:

The judge ruled in favor of the defendant, who owed the plaintiff nothing because the alarm was not installed correctly. (The plaintiff had not fulfilled the terms of the second half of their agreement.) The court also decided that the defendant could keep the system, which the other electricians had rewired correctly, and the judge advised the defendant to countersue for the loss and damages from the burglary.

## CHAPTER 6 / GOING PLACES

### Part One, Exercise D:

Many things can go wrong on a trip, but you can avoid the most common travel mistakes by gathering general and specific information in advance. Before you pay for a cruise, an organized tour, etc., be sure to ask questions about rules and refunds.

### Part Two, Exercise A:

Airline fares can be very confusing because there are so many different rates and special prices and because these change so frequently. Even travel agents have a hard time keeping up with the current bargains: travelers on the same flight may be paying several different rates, depending on when and from whom they bought their tickets and what restrictions they have complied with. In some cases, confused customers might decide to give up and to use some other form of transportation.

**Part Three, Exercise D:**

The following organization names and addresses are from the 1986 edition of the *Directory of Low Cost Vacations with a Difference*, compiled by J. Crawford, Pilot Industries, Inc., 103 Cooper Street, Babylon, New York 11702:

1. The International Home Exchange Service/ INTERVAC U.S., P.O. Box 3975, San Francisco CA 94119. (Specialties: home exchanges and visits)

2. American Youth Hostels, National Administrative Offices, 1332 "I" Street, NW, Suite 800, Washington DC 20005 (Specialties: inexpensive accommodations)

3. Bicycle U.S.A., Suite 209, 6707 Whitestone Road, Baltimore MD 21207. (Specialties: home stays, travel information, referrals to local bicycle clubs)

4. Bed and Breakfast Homes, Cape Breton Development Corporation, Box 13330, Sydney, Nova Scotia, Canada. (Specialties: home stays for paying guests as part of the Meet the Canadians at Home Program)

5. Servas, 11 John Street, Suite 706, New York NY 10038. (Specialties: worldwide, free hospitality for travelers to help build world peace)

6. Elderhostel, 80 Boylston Street, Suite 400, Boston MA 02116. (Specialties: educational and cultural courses for older people)

## CHAPTER 7 / Getting Along with People

**Part One, Exercise D:**

Younger people may have fewer preformed ideas about "appropriate" men's and women's work than older ones. But even older people who generally have traditional views on the roles of men and women may "change their minds" when doing so would be to their advantage—by helping them to avoid work, for example.

**Part Two, Exercise A:**

When people in a close relationship are angry or hurt, they tend to think the worst of each other. They focus on negative points or look at each other's characteristics in the most negative way possible. But when they realize they miss each other, they may forget all these negative thoughts.

## CHAPTER 8 / Having Fun

**Part Two, Exercise A:**

The husband has given his wife the responsibility of coming up with an activity they could enjoy together, but he's turned down every idea she's had and hasn't made any suggestions himself.

## CHAPTER 9 / The Media

**Part One, Exercise D:**

The story has two points. The speaker says that he opposes T.V. watching for many reasons, but like most people, he can get so involved in a program that he refuses to have it turned off. Also, the two roommates in the story aren't really talking or listening to each other because they are each absorbed in a different matter.

**Part Two, Exercise A:**

When the first roommate expresses her opinion about the shows that she considers of high quality and educational value, her roommate politely agrees. But when it comes to choosing programs to watch, the second speaker prefers to relax with shows that are less "demanding" to the brain.

## CHAPTER 10 / A Lifetime of Learning

**Part One, Exercise D:**

The speaker used several effective methods to learn her new language, but the most effective one will probably be getting personally involved in the culture by marrying an American.

**Part Two, Exercise A:**

Besides attending English class and completing assignments, there are many ways to improve your language skills, and you can discuss these methods with other students. Don't forget that people learn differently, and each individual will have to choose the methods that work best for him or her.